MW01504107

ZACH MITCHELL WOULD LIKE TO THANK

Jesus Christ

-

Thank You for Your unconditional love. Thank You for saving an imperfect person like me. Thank You for using me to share Your love into this broken world.

Debby

-

Thank you for your faith in me, your support, and your love. Thank you for doing this crazy adventure called life with me. Thank you for all the work you have put into this book! I couldn't do this without you!

Alex

-

Thank you for all the hard work you do for me, your support, your belief in me, and for making everything look awesome. Thank you for making the book cover and the book look amazing! Much love bro!

Big Mike

-

Thank you for standing strong, prevailing in life's hardships, and in your faith. Thank you for all of your love and support! You have taught me so much and inspired me in my faith. Always remember to trust God in the good times and in the bad times.

Zach and Brandi

-

Thank you for all of the hard work and the time that you put into this book. Thank you for challenging me and helping me grow as a writer. Most of all, thank you for your love and support!

Mom, Dad, and my brother Nick

Taylor - Thank you for your love and support!

Eric - Thank you for your friendship, your time, support, and love!

Thank you
-

Monte.
Connor.
Matt.
Scott.
Luke.
Joe and Ruth K.
Blurb Books.
Scooters Coffee.
Full Circle Book Coop.
Last Stop CD Shop.
Staples.
Crossroads Book and Music.

All my friends and family who love and support me!

Thank you to everyone who picked up this book, and supports Broken Worship. Your support makes my dream possible and encourages me to use my gifts for good.

I hope this book encourages you, challenges you, and blesses you in some way. Thank you!

TABLE OF CONTENTS

INTRODUCTION

Hello, my fellow reader. Thank you for starting a new journey with me. It is such a blessing to be a self-published author that gets to reach people with my work. In this journey through the pages of this book, we will be venturing through a variety of topics. We will really be hitting the topic of grace, why we desperately need this gift, and what we should do with this gift. We will be talking about the journey of faith and the sanctification process.

My life has been a process of never ending changes and growth, from overcoming a speech impediment, conquering a porn addiction, career changes, artistic changes and growth, overcoming abusing alcohol, to changes and growth in my faith journey. I have had my share of very dark lows to overwhelming highs.

I have gone through stages of wanting to hate God to complete reliance on God. There are times that I truly believe that I wouldn't be here today without God. I don't know where you stand in your life, your faith, your belief system, or your view of God. If you will journey with me through the pages of this book, I promise to give you a very vulnerable, truthful, and loving portrayal of God, grace, and what it means to have a life of faith. Just like the expression 'Rome wasn't built in a day,' the journey of faith truly takes a lifetime. There will be highs and there will be lows, but with God's grace, there will be growth. That growth looks different for everyone and every journey is unique.

To my readers that are not in the Christian faith, I want to express that I love you all and there is no judgment here. I'm writing this to express what I believe in and hopefully something I say makes sense. I do hope that if you decide to read on, that you read with an open mind and a soft heart. If you don't believe this to be your truth, I totally respect that and I'm just here to show love to you.

To my fellow Christian readers, I hope this book encourages you to remember how much we need God. We are nothing without God's grace. It doesn't matter what church you attend, or how much money you give to the church, or how many sermons you've listened to; we need a relationship with God. We need His grace. We need to look back on the life of Christ and how radical His life was. Jesus went to radical means to save you and we need to do radical things to love others. We aren't here to say that we believe in God and then invest in our own future. We need to genuinely love God and genuinely love people. That is what our lives should reflect- love. It's not about how many Bible verses you know, it's about how you treat others. I'm not saying that you shouldn't read your Bible, but ultimately it's about acting it out, and not keeping it in your safe Christian bubble. I hope that this book encourages you and challenges you to think about what a life of following God truly looks like.

I pray by the end of this book, we will more clearly understand how much God loves us. We are intensely loved by God. Loved enough to have Jesus come and live amongst us, teach us, and be the ultimate sacrifice.

We are to accept that gift and then share that gift with the whole world. We are loved by God and we are to be the light of God. I would like to add, throughout the book, I am using my personal interpretations and understanding of God's word. Thank you all for being willing to take this journey with me. Let's begin. I present you -

SAVING GRACE

IT'S NOT ABOUT YOU ANYMORE

CHAPTER ONE

WHAT IS GRACE AND WHY DO WE NEED IT?

John 3:16-21 (English Standard Version (ESV)- 2001- Crossway)

For God so loved the world, that He gave His only Son, that whoever believes in Him should not perish but have eternal life. For God did not send His Son into the world to condemn the world, but in order that the world might be saved through Him. Whoever believes in Him is not condemned, but whoever does not believe is condemned already, because he has not believed in the name of the only Son of God. And this is the judgment: the light has come into the world, and people loved the darkness rather than the light because their works were evil. For everyone who does wicked things hates the light and does not come to the light, lest his works should be exposed. But whoever does what is true comes to the light, so that it may be clearly seen that his works have been carried out in God.

Do you remember the classic Christmas movie 'A Christmas Story'? On the walk to school, Ralphie, his friends, and his little brother Randy, always encountered the town bully on the way home. Then one day, after Ralphie had a horrible day at school, he was feeling frustrated that he would not be getting his dream Christmas gift of a BB gun, and the bully started at it again. Ralphie finally had enough, so he tackled the bully down, punched and swore at him. The fight got vicious, and his mom came to pull him off of the bully. When they got home for supper, Ralphie and his brother, Randy, were crying that their dad was going to 'kill' Ralphie. When supper time came and their mom made light of the incident, it really impacted Ralphie. Ralphie thought he was going to get what he deserved for punching and swearing at a kid, but Ralphie's mom had shown an act of grace. I believe the Christian definition of grace, according to Oxford Languages on Google Dictionary, really hits the meaning of the term spot on, "the free and unmerited favor of God, as manifested in the salvation of sinners and the bestowal of blessings." In the beginning, God created a perfect and beautiful world. He also created Adam and Eve. They lived in the 'Garden of Eden', which was a paradise, pretty much 'Heaven on Earth'. They had everything they needed and an unfiltered relationship with God, their Creator. There was no death, no corruption of sin, everything was perfect. God didn't want to create self-serving robots, He gave us our own free will. He gave Adam and Eve a rule to live by. His command was, "You can enjoy everything beautiful and perfect that I created for you, but don't eat from the tree of 'Knowledge Of Good and Evil'." *(Paraphrased from Genesis 2:16-18.)* Then the adversary came as a serpent to tempt them. The devil gave them the idea that God was keeping something from them, and if they ate from that one tree, they could become more like God. With selfish desire, Adam and Eve gave into the devil's temptation and sin entered the world. I believe that all sin is rooted in selfishness. The desire to put ourselves above anything else. Lust, greed, envy, and idolatry are all rooted in how to make ourselves look and feel better. Like our own comfort and well-being are the most important things to us in this life. We are all guilty of it. When things aren't going our way, we say that life isn't fair. We have all asked the question, "How could there be a God when there is so much injustice in this world?"

What if there is a bigger question? How could we allow so much injustice? Why do we feel so entitled to the 'American Dream'? We think we must have the perfect romantic partner, the perfect job, the perfect house, beautiful children, perfect vacations, and a luxurious retirement. Instead of asking, "How could a good God allow starving kids in Africa or loved ones to die of cancer?" What if we asked the question, "What are we doing or where is our heart with this injustice?"

One thing I want to address is that everyone has sinned against a perfect God. We, like Adam and Eve, choose our selfishness instead of living in the perfect love of God. Due to our sin nature, we can not earn the love of God. Instead, God offers us a free gift of grace. If we accept this gift, we can inherit eternal life and spend eternity in the love of our Creator.

As the verse I stated at the beginning of the chapter says, God so loved us that He sent His only Son to die for us and save us from our sins. He not only came to die for us, but also showed us how to live. Not as some rich ruler, but as a servant. What these verses are also saying is that Jesus is the light of the world and the light shines through the darkness. There are people who are willing to confess their darkness to come towards the light; their darkness being their selfishness, their pride, and their desires. While others stray from the light, so that their darkness is not exposed, and they can stay in the life that they are living. I believe that in this life, we have one big question to answer: Will we accept the free gift of God, saving grace, be willing to come to the light, to give up our sinful ways, and to walk in the love of Christ, or will we choose our sinful desires (selfishness, pride, greed, envy, lust) and hide from the light? I believe that is life's biggest and most important question.

Romans 3:10-12 (English Standard Version (ESV)- 2001- Crossway)
"None is righteous, no, not one; no one understands; no one seeks for God. All have turned aside; together they have become worthless; no one does good, not even one."

I have always believed, when reflecting on life and the world around us, every one of us in the depths of our being, believes that this world and each one of us in it was created with a purpose. We know we make mistakes and we just don't measure up, but then we tell ourselves, "Well, so and so has messed up way more than me." In order to justify ourselves, we point out the crazy political climate, Hitler, and Putin, the Russian dictator who attacked the country of Ukraine. We then justify our actions, because there are people who have done worse than us. As the Bible verse in Romans says, "No one is good, no, not one." No one measures up to God's perfect standards. Due to our inherently selfish nature, we can't justify ourselves just because someone is worse than us. We have sinned against the perfect God that created us. Just like we know Putin should be punished for his crimes, a perfect and just God can't let a crime go unpunished. God loves us all. He loves you just as much as He loves Putin, the Russian dictator. We are all made in God's image. He loves us all so much, to the point of sacrificing His only Son to die for us, who paid the ultimate sacrifice, so that we can be saved from what we deserve.

I grew up in a loving, Christian home. I was blessed with parents who loved me and my siblings. They worked hard to provide for us. They taught my siblings and I the importance of God, His love for us, and also the importance of obeying His commandments. Even though my faith differs from my parents, I am beyond grateful for the way I was raised. Beginning in my teenage years, I started to rebel, which led to a severe porn addiction, severely abusing alcohol, and a life of partying. I hurt a lot of people in those times. I always had to get drunk and I gave into sinful desires. I am ashamed of my past, but I am so grateful for God's grace and mercy in my life. Through the mess, and not the purest start of the relationship, I found my girlfriend, who deeply loves me and pushes me to be better every day. I started back on my faith journey and the sanctification process. There have been times that I wanted to hate God in my lowest lows, but God always showed up for me. There were times that all I could do was to rely on God. I know that the path that I was on was spiritually, mentally, physically, and emotionally killing me. But praise be to God for always loving me through my mistakes. I knew my ministry was for loving the outcasts and the marginalized. Religion has pushed so many away, but God wants a relationship with you. He wants your mess, He can handle it. He just needs you to be open, honest, and to be in the light of Christ.

Through the rest of this book, I am going to address God's radical love for us and our commandment from Him to radically love others. Just as we do not deserve grace, but were freely given it, our command is to truly give grace to others. We will be talking about the journey of faith, how it is not an overnight journey, but a lifelong process of sanctification and reliance on God. Let's keep going on this journey together!

CHAPTER TWO

THE RADICAL LOVE OF JESUS

Luke 5:1-11 (English Standard Version (ESV)- 2001- Crossway)

On one occasion, while the crowd was pressing in on Him to hear the word of God, He was standing by the lake of Gennesaret, and He saw two boats by the lake, but the fishermen had gone out of them and were washing their nets. Getting into one of the boats, which was Simon's, He asked him to put out a little from the land. And He sat down and taught the people from the boat. And when He had finished speaking, He said to Simon, "Put out into the deep and let down your nets for a catch." And Simon answered, "Master, we toiled all night and took nothing!

But at Your word I will let down the nets." And when they had done this, they enclosed a large number of fish, and their nets were breaking. They signaled to their partners in the other boat to come and help them. And when Simon Peter saw it, he fell down at Jesus' knees, saying, "Depart from me, for I am a sinful man, O Lord." For he and all who were with him were astonished at the catch of fish that they had taken, and so also were James and John, sons of Zebedee, who were partners with Simon. And Jesus said to Simon, "Do not be afraid; from now on you will be catching men."And when they had brought their boats to land, they left everything and followed Him.

For my fellow football fans, I want you to imagine a scenario. You're a football coach for an incredible, small town, high school football team. You've coached this team for 20 years. You are the most respected coach and have the most respected team throughout the league. This year, you have built the best team you have had in all of the 20 years that you have been coaching. You have the most accurate Quarterback, the fastest Running Back, and two of the strongest Wide Receivers. You have had an undefeated season and you are preparing for the championship game. Now, you also have a smaller sized kid on your team that all of the players make fun of and push around. You, as a coach, are even guilty of making jokes at him, because he is so small and considered weird. The kid always asks to be able to play a game as a Running Back. Everyone always laughs at him and tells him, "Yeah, in your wildest dreams!" The kid does his very best to try to please the team. He acts as the waterboy, always sets up the practice field, and cleans everything up after practices and games. He still gets laughed at and taken advantage of. Now, the night before the championship game, the starting Quarterback, Running Back, and the two Wide Receivers were partying it up and got into a car accident. The Quarterback and one of the Wide Receivers got pretty banged up, but sadly the Running Back and the other Wide Receiver passed away. So, for the championship game, all hope has been lost. The Quarterback was not in good shape, there was no starting Running Back, and only one Wide Receiver, who was also pretty banged up. In the game, the team's offense was getting destroyed, and the only reason they were staying in the game is because of their strong defense. After getting their butts handed to them in the first half of the game, you, as the coach, finally let the little kid come in as Running Back. After all hope had been lost, and the ball was handed to the kid, every person in the stadium went silent. This kid ran for a 74 yard touchdown, bypassing all the big and aggressive players, outrunning every player on the field. Once he got the touchdown, everyone just stopped for a minute in awe. You, as the coach, ran up to him and gave him a hug. For the rest of the game, the kid started every play, and your team managed to win the championship. At the end of the game, you went to him to apologize for all the mistreatment he had received and the unwillingness you had to put your faith in him. You then rewarded him with the game ball.

Going back to the set of verses I shared at the beginning of the chapter, fishing was everything to Simon. Being a fisherman was his trade, his career. He had to be an expert at it. Times were tough and I'm sure he wasn't a millionaire by any means. He stayed out in that lake all night and didn't catch a single fish. He then saw this Jesus character in the morning, preaching to a crowd of people. While Simon was cleaning up his nets, after a long and disappointing night, Jesus got into Simon's boat and continued preaching. He then asked Simon to go back out and cast his nets again. Simon must have thought, the audacity of this Jesus guy, who must He think He is? This was Simon's trade, and like he said, he was out there all night and didn't catch a single fish. But because Simon had heard about Jesus, there must have been enough respect there and maybe some desperation, Simon went ahead and listened to Jesus. Boy, oh boy, did that act of obedience pay off for Simon. The nets were breaking, he had to get his partner's boat and there was enough fish to start sinking two boats. I have to think Jesus must have gotten a kick out of that. This was not only meeting Simon's needs, but overly exceeding his needs and his wildest expectations. Jesus did not only know Simon, but loved Simon more than Simon could have ever imagined. I believe Jesus went over the top with the amount of fish that He gave to Simon, not only to exceed Simon's expectations, but just to show the amount of how much Jesus loved Simon. More love than we could ever imagine.

Jesus loves us so much more than we could ever imagine. Not only does He love us, but He knows us. He knows our story, He knows the desire of our hearts. He knows our frustrations, our hardships, and our heartaches. He knows it all. He knows when it feels like life isn't fair and when it all feels hopeless. He loves us through the hardships and trials of this life. He then does not only meet, but often exceeds our needs. The last part of the Scriptures says that after Jesus provided an over abundance of fish, He then says Simon would become a fisher of men. You might be asking, what does that even mean, 'Fisher of men'?

That is a call to reach people for Jesus. We need Christ's love more than we need food to eat, an income, a job/career, more than anything. That is why Simon and his partners left the two boats of fish to follow Jesus. Simon recognized how Holy Jesus was and that he, himself, was a sinner not worthy of Jesus. All that Simon knew was that he needed what Jesus had to offer. By leaving the boats behind, it was symbolic of leaving his sinful and selfish ways of living behind. He wanted to live in the light and love of Christ. That is what Jesus commands of us, to believe in Him, give up our old ways, and live a new life. It's not about ourselves anymore. Obedience leads to spiritual growth. We will never be truly satisfied in our own ways. We know what it's like to live day after day with hardships and trials, and to never feel hope, or to see the light at the end of the tunnel. That is what Jesus showed Simon, and that is what He is showing us here today. He is the way out. He is the answer. He is our hope and our future. To be 'fishers of men', we need to share that hope with others. We need to share the hope of the Gospel message and the good news of Jesus Christ.

When we accept the gift of God's grace and love, we can't keep that to ourselves. Jesus' ministry was to show us the way to live in love and we are supposed to carry that out.

John 7:53-8:11 (English Standard Version (ESV)- 2001- Crossway)

They went each to his own house, but Jesus went to the Mount of Olives. Early in the morning He came again to the temple. All the people came to Him, and He sat down and taught them. The Scribes and the Pharisees brought a woman who had been caught in adultery, and placing her in the midst they said to Him, "Teacher, this woman has been caught in the act of adultery. Now in the Law, Moses commanded us to stone such women. So what do you say?" This they said to test Him, that they might have some charge to bring against Him. Jesus bent down and wrote with His finger on the ground. And as they continued to ask Him, He stood up and said to them, "Let him who is without sin among you be the first to throw a stone at her." And once more He bent down and wrote on the ground. But when they heard it, they went away one by one, beginning with the older ones, and Jesus was left alone with the woman standing before Him. Jesus stood up and said to her, "Woman, where are they? Has no one condemned you?" She said, "No one, Lord." and Jesus said, "Neither do I condemn you; go, and from now on sin no more."

I love this set of verses. I will say for you, the reader's knowledge, that these verses are said not to be a part of the original manuscripts of the Bible, but I love the message of this story. This woman obviously has not had an easy life, she has made her fair share of mistakes. Life caught up with her, and in the eyes of the law, she has been condemned to death. Talk about feeling hopeless and alone. Everyone in her life judged her and left her. She had definitely made mistakes, but I feel like her life was one hardship after another. She was always seen in her flaws and her mistakes, but Jesus saw something more in her. He saw her for who she really was- broken and hopeless. He loved her despite her flaws. He also knew the human condition, we are all sinful in the eyes of God and no one, no matter their status, is above the law. I have heard these sets of verses a lot in my life, and it always kept me wondering, what is it that Jesus wrote in the sand? It must have been something very thought-provoking. After He wrote in the sand, Jesus made a very bold and thought-provoking statement that even kept the Scribes and the Pharisees silent, "Let him who is without sin among you be the first to throw a stone at her." No one could refute that they had sinned. It personalized and maybe even put themselves in the woman's shoes. Probably for a minute, they thought, what if this was me? They then tossed the stones on the ground and one by one left the scene, leaving only Jesus and the woman. Can you imagine what this woman must have been feeling, after she was certain she was going to be stoned to death for her sins? There are no words that could describe that feeling. She has just been saved and forgiven by the Savior. From this moment on, every moment of her life is a gift from God. Not saying that there weren't hardships from that point on in this woman's life, but the perspective change that must have happened, the hard times don't look so bleak now. Nothing could be worse than if she had been stoned to death that day. Jesus, at the end of this story, tells the woman that He doesn't condemn her. This means that He does not judge her by her past. She has a new start. She also has a commandment to go on and sin no more. Now, obviously, from that point on she wasn't perfect, but she started a new journey that day. A journey of rebirth, a journey of faith and repentance. She knew the meaning of this life isn't about the mistakes from her past, or what she could do to save herself, but that there is a Savior that deeply loves her and saved her from condemnation. She was shown what saving grace is and will share it with others.

Luke 19:1-10 (English Standard Version (ESV)- 2001- Crossway)
He entered Jericho and was passing through. And there was a man named Zacchaeus. He was a tax collector and was rich. And he was seeking to see who Jesus was, but on

account of the crowd he could not, because he was small of stature. So he ran on ahead and climbed up into a sycamore tree to see Him, for He was about to pass that way. And when Jesus came to the place, He looked up and said to him, "Zacchaeus, hurry and come down, for I must stay at your house today." So he hurried and came down and received Him joyfully. And when they saw it, they all grumbled, "He has gone in to be the guest of a man who is a sinner." And Zacchaeus stood and said to the Lord, "Behold, Lord, the half of my goods I give to the poor. And if I have defrauded anyone of anything, I restore it fourfold." And Jesus said to him, "Today salvation has come to this house, since he also is a son of Abraham. For the Son of Man came to seek and to save the lost."

This is an awesome story of a change of heart and the love that Jesus has for the lost. Zacchaeus was in probably the most hated profession of that time. Tax collectors worked for the Roman government and collected ridiculous amounts of money from the poor, to ensure the reign of Rome. Even though Zacchaeus was a successful tax collector and was rich, he must have known that he was missing something in his life. He may have had the riches, but something was tormenting his soul. He knew that he needed more in this life. He then heard about this Jesus guy, who had performed miracles, could forgive sins, and save souls. This sounded like a guy Zacchaeus needed to meet. Maybe this was his 'light' at the end of the dark tunnel, that was his life. He finally had a glimpse of hope. I imagine Zacchaeus as this funny, short, chubby dude that was so annoyed because all of these tall people were blocking his view of Jesus. Since he was stubborn and a smart guy, he was going to go climb this tree ahead of everyone. That may not have been the best idea because he was short and chubby, but dang it, he needed to see this Jesus guy! When he finally saw Jesus, Jesus acknowledged Zacchaeus and actually wanted to meet with him. What an honor! Then something really discouraging happened, people are telling Jesus that He shouldn't have anything to do with him, because he is a sinner. But, because Zacchaeus really had a change of heart and wanted to follow Jesus, he had decided to give up his riches and give them to the poor. He was hoping to make up for all the wrong that he had committed against people. Jesus saw his change of heart and accepted him. Jesus loved Zacchaeus. Jesus intentionally sought Zacchaeus out to meet with him. Despite what people thought of Zacchaeus, Jesus loved him. He is here to seek and save the lost. He knows your past and still loves you. He is here to meet with you and to give you the hope of salvation. He wants to give us a new heart, a new hope, and a future. No matter what you have done, no matter how lost you are, Jesus wants to seek you out and have a meeting with you. He wants a relationship with you. He wants to be your Savior. Jesus knows your imperfections, He knows your story, He knows your shortcomings, and He radically loves you. He didn't come to condemn you, but to give you hope and a future. He came to die for each and every one of our sins, so that we can spend eternity with Him.

A few years ago, I ended up getting arrested for drunk driving. It was one of the scariest moments of my life. At that time in my life, I was drinking heavily and the drunk level that I was at was nothing new to me, which made me feel like I was comfortable to drive. I had no self-control. I was selfish and needed to chase that next level of drunkenness. Not only was that night scary for me, but it was scary and so emotionally damaging to my girlfriend and our best friend. I really hurt them, along with members of my family. I also knew that there were consequences to my actions and I knew that after sitting in jail for almost a whole day, that this was not who I wanted to be. I don't want to be that person in and out of the system, with two to three DUIs and having to go blow every day. I knew I needed to change. The guilt that I had was tremendous. After all of that, I knew God's grace was with me. I did not end up getting the DUI on my record and I did not lose my license. It was just a lot of money dealing with lawyer and court fees. God truly looked over me. By God's grace, the love and support of my girlfriend, friends, and family, continuing on the journey of my faith, and the sanctification process, I learned the importance of self-control. I learned that there are so many more important things in life, rather than chasing the next level of drunk. I still enjoy having a couple of beers or having a couple of drinks with my girlfriend, but thank God that I am not the person I was.

CHAPTER THREE

A SERVANT'S HEART

Matthew 25:35-46 (English Standard Version (ESV)- 2001- Crossway)

"For I was hungry and you gave Me food, I was thirsty and you gave Me drink, I was a stranger and you welcomed Me, I was naked and you clothed Me, I was sick and you visited Me, I was in prison and you came to Me.' Then the righteous will answer Him, saying, "Lord, when did we see You hungry and feed You, or thirsty and give You drink? And when did we see You sick or in prison and visit You?' And the King will answer them, 'Truly, I say to you, as you did it to one of the least of these my brothers, you did it to Me.' "Then He will say to those on His left, 'Depart from Me, you cursed, into the eternal fire prepared for the Devil and his angels. For I was hungry and you gave Me no food, I was thirsty and you gave Me no drink, I was a stranger and you did not welcome Me, naked and you did not clothe Me, sick and in prison and you did not visit Me.' Then they also will answer, saying, 'Lord, when did we see You hungry or thirsty or a stranger or naked or sick or in prison, and did not minister to You?' Then He will answer them, saying, 'Truly, I say to you, as you did not do it to one of the least of these, you did not do it to Me.' And these will go away into the eternal punishment, but the righteous into eternal life."

I know these verses are repetitive, but I absolutely love them and believe that they are one of the most vital sets of verses to our Christian faith. They are simple, but so direct. What this set of verses isn't emphasizing is how many times you went to church, or what good deeds you have done for the community, or how strong your faith is. What it's simply saying is that what you do for the least of these, which are the poor, the helpless, the sick, the imprisoned, you do for Jesus. When you avoid, judge, or harm the least of these, you do that to Jesus. These verses are not saying that helping the least of these is just a good idea. Eternity is on the line. You are commanded to have a heart for the people who are less fortunate than yourself.

You are to have a heart for the outcasts and the marginalized. When we are tempted to look at the homeless as lazy and drug-addicted bums, we are saying that of Jesus. When we look at the elderly and disabled and turn them a blind eye, we are overlooking Jesus. When we look at the people in the LGBTQ community and label them as sinful, weird, and not even give them a chance, we are doing that to Jesus. When we see inmates or criminals and automatically believe that they are the worst humans, without taking time to understand the specific situations, you are doing that to Jesus. I know that one person can't end the problems of homelessness, take in every refugee, or help every person in need. I believe there are people in everyone's life where it is easier to bypass them, rather than to take the time to talk to that person, listen to their story, and see if there is anything, big or small, that you could do for them. You would be surprised how a little listening goes a long way. It also doesn't have to be limited to just the homeless or marginalized communities. Every single person has a story waiting to be heard by a listening ear. Every person on this planet is dealing with an internal battle that is weighing on them, and it is so important to slow down and look for the moments that God puts in front of you, for you to bless someone in some way. I'm trying not to get too political with this book, but there are some things I need to address. When we care more about our rights and our freedoms, while judging someone that is taking COVID-19 seriously, and judging them for wearing a face mask, or for getting the COVID-19 vaccine, how is that loving? The COVID-19 pandemic has truly killed and affected the lives of so many people. Thinking people are crazy, or being a puppet to the media, is not what Jesus is commanding of us. We need to love and respect them, even if you aren't in the demographic of COVID-19 being fatal to you, or believe it's giving up your freedoms. Also, with the pro-life community, I see a lot of loud noises from them. So many pro-lifers think that it's evil to be pro-choice and will judge them. I believe it is our responsibility to take a step back and listen. Listen to the lost and hurting females. It's not like they are running to go get as many abortions as they possibly can. They are more often than not hurt, lost, judged, and alone. Take the time to listen to them, and hear their story.

James 1:19-20 (English Standard Version (ESV)- 2001- Crossway)
Know this, my beloved brothers: let every person be quick to hear, slow to speak, slow to anger; for the anger of man does not produce the righteousness of God.

We need to learn to see people with love and not

judgment. We, as Christians, have been redeemed, not because we deserved it, but because of God's deep love for us through His saving grace.

John 3:12-17 (English Standard Version (ESV)- 2001- Crossway)
When He had washed their feet and put on His outer garments and resumed His place, He said to them, "Do you understand what I have done to you? You call me Teacher and Lord, and you are right, for so I am. If I then, your Lord and Teacher, have washed your feet, you also ought to wash one another's feet. For I have given you an example, that you also should do just as I have done to you. Truly, truly, I say to you, a servant is not greater than his master, nor is a messenger greater than the one who sent him. If you know these things, blessed are you if you do them.

Can you imagine the President of the United States holding a political rally with a bowl of soapy water and a sponge, and going around to every person at the rally washing their feet? I can imagine former President Trump making some obnoxious, but still kind of funny, comment about how dehumanizing washing feet is, and we as Americans are too great for that. All jokes aside, there is no way a huge political leader would stoop so low, but that is exactly what our Savior did for His disciples. Feet aren't pretty. They are smelly, dirty, sweaty, and just disgusting.

Jesus again goes to radical lengths to show His love for us, and again commands that we go to radical lengths to show love for others. I know that in today's culture, we aren't actually washing each other's feet. I think with this commandment that Jesus gave us, it is more about serving others in ways that are vulnerable and meaningful. We shouldn't be afraid of getting our hands dirty when helping others. If that means helping an elderly couple clean their bathroom, or doing dishes for a disabled person. Don't be so prideful that you can't be willing to do something that might get your hands dirty.

I have a heart for people with disabilities. I believe this stems from when I was a child and I struggled with a speech impediment. I've discussed this in my previous books, but the doctors told my parents that I should learn sign language, because they didn't think that I was going to be able to speak. By the grace of God and my parents pushing me, I powered through and did learn to speak. My girlfriend works with a company that takes care of disabled individuals. The job is tough physically, mentally, emotionally, and spiritually, but the people she takes care of are beautiful souls. I have had the privilege of getting to know three of them. Some of them have Down syndrome, others have different types of disabilities, but I always look forward to seeing them and I have grown to love them. I know that there are people who don't treat them right, or do their best to avoid them, because they are different, but they have blessed my life and they have blessed my girlfriend's. I know that having a relationship with someone with a mental disability takes some knowledge and time, but please be kind to them and greet them with a warm "Hello" and "How are you." One of my favorite movies titled, 'The Peanut Butter Falcon', is about a guy with Down syndrome named Zak. He has a passion and desire to be a professional wrestler and dreams of meeting his wrestling hero. There is also another guy, who hasn't had an easy life and is always on the run, because he's committing crimes to survive. Zak and the other character, named Tyler, eventually run into each other and go on an adventure to meet Zak's hero, the professional wrestler named 'The Salt Water Redneck'. It's a beautiful story showing how a person with Down syndrome has hopes, dreams, and how they want to be treated like everyone else.

The last thing I want to bring up is about what my family is going through with my grandma. My grandma, who is my mom's mom, struggles with dementia, which is a condition of memory loss. She has gone downhill fast within the last few years. It is tough watching her go through this and it really puts valuing our mental consciousness in a whole new perspective. Our family has been visiting her in a memory care facility for a few years now. I have tried to go help her eat her lunches. It really hurts seeing her now, because she was such a strong woman and pretty stubborn, but to this day, she has a great heart. We recently had to move her into a nursing home, which was a tough transition. I don't know how much she knows about what's going on, or what she is aware of, but I know I love her and want to help by giving her my time.

To wrap up this chapter, having a servant's heart does not always seem to be in our nature, but it is the most vital role in our faith. It is not always easy, and we won't be perfect at it. God doesn't expect perfection, He knows that we aren't perfect. He wants us to walk with Him. I will be discussing in another chapter about the journey of faith and the sanctification process. Just remember, we are deeply and radically loved by God. We are to love God and love people. When we have our hearts and our lives focused on loving God and loving His creation, that is when our lives will be more satisfying. Focusing on ourselves and our selfish desires will never truly satisfy. It is when we are living in God's will and when we bless others, that our hearts will be content and our lives will be Spirit-filled.

CHAPTER FOUR

FAITH IS A JOURNEY

THE SANCTIFICATION PROCESS

Romans 7:15-20 (English Standard Version (ESV)- 2001- Crossway)

For I do not understand my own actions. For I do not do what I want, but I do the very thing I hate. Now if I do what I do not want, I agree with the law, that it is good. So now it is no longer I who do it, but sin that dwells within me. For I know that nothing good dwells in me, that is, in my flesh. For I have the desire to do what is right, but not the ability to carry it out. For I do not do the good I want, but the evil I do not want is what I keep on doing. Now if I do what I do not want, it is no longer I who do it, but sin that dwells within me.

Have you ever been addicted to something? An addiction usually starts as something you enjoy, but then turns into something you need and it can destroy you. Whether that be taking a hit of something at a party or looking at something you know you shouldn't, then the next thing you know you can't stop and it controls you. Addiction is a powerful and scary thing. Addiction can lead to depression and anxiety which amplifies the 'need' of the addiction.

I think addiction and sin, especially in this set of verses, really coincide with each other. I know this set of verses can seem wordy and confusing, but what it's basically saying is that the author, whose name is Paul, has a desire to do what is right, but his sin nature defeats his desire to do what is right. It is a constant battle. We try our absolute hardest to do what is right, but it is so easy and feels inevitable to give into our desires. Due to my past, I know I would not be able to change without the love of God and my loved ones. I have learned about myself, that I don't like being by myself for large amounts of time and I have to keep busy. I think being alone with my thoughts is not good for my battle with depression and anxiety. There are times that I don't think very highly of myself and I get wrapped up in all of my past failures, and that is really not good for me. My girlfriend and I have recently launched a new residential cleaning company to service homes in small South Dakota towns that aren't near big cities. My girlfriend has had to keep her full-time job for income while I am trying to get the business off the ground. I took a huge leap of faith leaving my full-time job to start a dream endeavor of owning our own business. I have never really known what I wanted to do with my life, career wise. So many people go to college after high school to pursue a degree and pretty much have their career planned out for them. I have always been kind of different. I always wanted to pursue God and my dreams through art. I started with a metal band called 'Rebuild The Fallen' and then ventured into poetry and writing. I always knew I could work at our family business, which was a magazine and book wholesaler. It was a lot of work and a lot of hours on the road, driving to towns all over South Dakota, even venturing into Minnesota and Iowa, to set up magazines and books on shelves in grocery stores and other businesses. It was hard work, a lot of hours, but I was good at it. It was really good for me financially, and I could always rely on it. But then, my now brother-in-law, provided me with a new opportunity that sounded like it was a great path for a career with great benefits as a custodian. I decided to go for it for a change. I learned a lot. There were some very humbling experiences as a custodian, I worked hard and I really liked and befriended everyone I worked with. When my girlfriend and I bought a house, about an hour's drive away, and the pay didn't make it feel worth the long drive, on top of always feeling so busy and not being able to actually spend time with my girlfriend, I knew something needed to change. With my experience, my girlfriend's hard work ethic, and attention to detail, I really believed that we could start a residential cleaning service in these small towns. Like I said, it took a huge leap of faith, and things haven't been easy, at times even scary, but we believe it can work and it will be a huge blessing. We also believe that God knows the desire of our hearts, and if we seek Him first, He will meet our needs.

I think the faith journey looks a lot like that. It takes a huge leap of faith to give up your wants, your desires, and decide to put your whole heart and all of your trust in Jesus. It can be a scary decision, but in your heart of hearts, you know that what you're doing isn't working. Your sins, your desires, your path is leading to a dead end and you need hope, you need love, and you need to be saved. The decision to put your faith in Jesus is scary, but it is so beyond worth it. When you decide to take the leap, you are forgiven and your soul is as white as snow on judgment day. Jesus paid your debt before an all knowing, perfect, and just God, so that you are seen as worthy as God's only Son. After you take the leap of faith and accept the gift of grace, you are given a new heart, and new desires, but things don't change overnight. You will still struggle and you will still have temptations. What is different is that now you are walking in relationship with Jesus and you can reach out to Him for help. We will never be perfect in this life, but with the gift of grace, we are given new desires. We desire to love God and serve others. We know we aren't saved based on what we did to deserve it, but because of what Jesus has done for us. That leads us into the sanctification process. Even when we take one step forward and two steps back, we learn from our mistakes and learn to lean on God. We now have a desire to obey God and follow His commandments. We learn to have a heart for others and want others to experience the love and the hope of Jesus. One of the absolute best ways of getting close and having a relationship with Jesus is reading the Word of God, the Bible. As I have discussed in my third book, 'Imperfectly Spreading A Perfect Gospel', you need to have a respect and understanding of how to read the Bible. There are different authors and it is written to different groups of people, but the Bible is God inspired and God breathed. With time and effort, we get to start learning and growing in our faith. Reading the Bible is just like the journey of faith, it takes time and effort, but it will produce growth.

2 Corinthians 12:9 (English Standard Version (ESV)- 2001- Crossway)
But He said to me, "My grace is sufficient for you, for My power is made perfect in weakness." Therefore I will boast all the more gladly of my weaknesses, so that the power of Christ may rest upon me.

Have you ever wondered how a perfect God could even use a broken mess like me? You may think that you are not the smartest, the most creative, the most outspoken, the strongest, or gifted person. You may also think that you have too much of a past for God to use you or even for anyone to take you seriously. I won't get into too many details, but I am going to take a bit to describe some people in my life who have overcome traumatic pasts and found faith. Their journeys are nowhere near perfect, and they still struggle, but by God's love and God's grace, they have made a difference in this world and they have made a difference in my life.

My girlfriend did not have an easy past. She grew up in Oklahoma. Her father and then also her step-father were alcoholics. Her step-dad abused her mother. She remembers guarding her little brother's eyes as her mom was being abused by her step-dad, and then she had to clean up the blood. When she was in high school, she was molested by some of the school's football team. There was much more in her past, but the point is that she had a traumatic life growing up. She then married her high school sweetheart, but it ended up not working out because he wanted her to sleep with his friends. She then met her second husband, they moved to Minnesota and raised a beautiful family with awesome pets, but they grew out of love because it ended up being all about money for her ex-husband. Through Debby's adult life, she did have a lot of hardships, but she always had a heart for others. She believed in her daughter's ministry, which led them to knowing a lot of awesome Christian rappers, evangelists, and having a heart for the African community. She touched the hearts of so many struggling Africans and helped support them financially and spiritually. She also has an amazing son. Her son faces some disabilities after witnessing the traumatic injury of his sister as they grew up. He has some hardships, but he has such a great heart and is so loving. When we met, she saw my heart and she guided me, taught me, loved me, and blessed me in more ways than words can explain. She has the purest heart and lives in the love of God.

My friend also had a traumatic past. He has always struggled with a mental disability and bipolar disorder, which was really hard for him growing up. He also was a rape victim at a very young age. Unfortunately, he wasn't just raped once in his life. He faced encounters from a child through his high school years. It really affected him. From a young age, he suffered from being a rape victim, to being mistreated for his mental disabilities, and also for being bisexual. By the grace of God, my friend found Jesus. It took him a lot of time, but from the point where he found Jesus, he had a new heart and a new love for people. He was slowly able to start forgiving and healing from the incidents of his past. I believe that God put him in my life for a purpose. I believe I was able to encourage him and help strengthen him in his faith. He was also there for me through some of the toughest times in my life. There were times where I felt everyone walked away from me, but my friend didn't. He loved me, fought for me, and stuck by me. Even if he doesn't always understand this, he truly showed me Christ's love when I desperately needed it. My girlfriend and I love him so much and he has become family to us.

The last story I wanted to mention is from another best friend of mine. He has always been the odd-one-out, the outcast. Growing up with a broken home, and a family of small town 'hicks', he was the metalhead. He ended up going through a phase of drugs, alcohol, and partying. Through that stage, he started dating a girl who ended up cheating on him, came back, and then gave him a lifelong STD. He always had and still has the deep desire to get married and have kids, and that has definitely been a huge setback for him. As he got older, even through the hardships of his past, he knew that he wanted to strive to be better. Even though, due to his past, he had to drop out of high school, he managed to get a GED, while working a full time job and dealing with depression, anxiety, and a really tough and failing relationship. He also managed to buy his family's mobile home that he grew up in, with cash, which was a huge life accomplishment. Then when life started looking positive and things were turning around, life gave him some more curveballs. He ended up getting a huge digestive disorder from eating undercooked food, which will stay with him for the rest of his life. On top of everything, due to the land that his mobile home set on being sold, he then had to spend a big portion of his hard earned savings to move his mobile home to a different trailer court. He felt like he was on ground zero again financially. Being the person that he is, he never gave up. He has continued to work hard, worked on new dietary plans, and is still pursuing his dreams of music. He has started a food and beverage review page, and is still holding on to hope that he will one day be married and have kids. My friend is unsure of where he stands in his faith, but he overcame so much, all by his own blood, sweat, and tears, and I believe that God is working on his heart.

2 Corinthians 7:10 (English Standard Version (ESV)- 2001- Crossway)
For Godly grief produces a repentance that leads to salvation without regret, whereas worldly grief produces death.

I know how easy it is to be weighed down by guilt and regret. I also know how it feels like you will never be good enough, strong enough, or worthy enough. It is so easy to let yourself down, let others down, and be overcome by hurt and guilt. We are imperfect humans. I love my family and I know they love me, but sometimes I feel like they criticize my every move and that I will never be good enough. It really affects me when my mom and I get into it. I know that she wants what is best for me, but I have to realize that I will never meet all of her expectations and that I have to continue to strive to do my best. I can't compare my life with how other people are living their lives. My younger sister went to school for nursing and is now an active nurse with an amazing husband, who is seriously one of my best friends in this world, and who is also named Zach, haha. Zachs tend to be pretty awesome! Anyway, as a couple they make great money, get to go on awesome vacations, and are well off. I am so proud of them, but I can't compare how my life is going in comparison with them, because that's not me.

Going back to the latest verse I just shared, being weighed down by guilt and shame will only lead to depression, anxiety, and to the extreme of no self-worth, that can lead to suicidal thoughts and even death.
Living in that is living in caged torment. But in the eyes of being saved by grace, it helps you know where you have fallen short, you know that you are forgiven, that you are not condemned by your mistakes, and that you can lean on God to help improve in the areas that you have been lacking in. I want to make this very clear, if you are a Christian, or if you are not a person of faith, you are more than your mistakes. You are so deeply loved by God and by people. Sometimes people aren't the best at sharing love, but no matter what you are facing, you are worth more than whatever it is that you are facing. You are deeply loved.

Romans 6:1-4 (English Standard Version (ESV)- 2001- Crossway)

What shall we say then? Are we to continue in sin that grace may abound? By no means! How can we who died to sin still live in it? Do you not know that all of us who have been baptized into Christ Jesus were baptized into His death? We were buried therefore with Him by baptism into death, in order that, just as Christ was raised from the dead by the glory of the Father, we too might walk in newness of life.

Romans 7:7-12 (English Standard Version (ESV)- 2001- Crossway)

What then shall we say? That the law is sin? By no means! Yet if it had not been for the law, I would not have known sin. For I would not have known what it is to covet if the law had not said, "You shall not covet." But sin, seizing an opportunity through the commandment, produced in me all kinds of covetousness. For apart from the law, sin lies dead. I was once alive apart from the law, but when the commandment came, sin came alive and I died. The very commandment that promised life proved death to me. For sin, seizing an opportunity through the commandment, deceived me and through it killed me. So the law is holy, and the commandment is holy and righteous and good.

There are some common misconceptions about being saved by grace. Oftentimes, people go too far in one direction or the other. Some people think that since Jesus died for all of their sins, they can pretty much do whatever they want. It's already been paid for so they want to take advantage of it. What the first set of the verses that I just shared is saying, well hold up, yes you are saved and your sins are forgiven, but if you are a Christian, just like Jesus died for your sins, you are to die to sin and have a new heart. When you are saved, you are to be born again, you give up your sinful desires and seek to follow Jesus, love others, and obey His commandments. If you think that it's just a free pass to do whatever you want and to get away with it, you have missed the point. Being saved by grace does not mean you will be perfect, but it starts a new journey for you. The new journey is your personal, spiritual walk with Jesus, learning and building a relationship with Him. This path, or journey, takes a lifetime and does not happen overnight, and you will struggle, but you grow and you become more sanctified with every step of the journey. Just like a romantic relationship, it is exciting at first, sparks fly, but it does take work and effort to keep the relationship going and to grow in it. It won't always be butterflies and daisies. There will be tough and difficult moments, but Jesus will never walk away and He will always be there to pick you up when you fall.

On the other end of the spectrum, there are people who think that once you have become a Christian, you are to be perfect. They believe that there is no room for error. They will give you a judgmental eye if a swear word comes out of your mouth, or if they ever see you with a beer in hand. This mindset is very common in 'religious' practices. They often want to seem 'holier' than everyone around them. They want to seem like they have their act together. Because I know that no one is perfect, when I come across someone like this, I tend to think that they are hiding something. Maybe they do have their 'poop in a group', but the most important aspect of the Christian faith is love and that we are not the judge. Only God is the true and just Judge. So, if you or someone you know falls into this mindset, remember we are not the judge. Our call as Christians is to love others. If you do see someone messing up, the first thing you should do is listen and encourage. Don't shove things or judgment down their throat. Build a relationship with that person and show them the love of Jesus. We can speak out against evil or injustice without spreading hate. Remember that every person and every journey is different. We don't know what someone is going through and others don't know what we are going through. Remember, a journey with God starts with a heart change and we can't change a heart, but we can point people to the One who can.

John 16:33 (English Standard Version (ESV)- 2001- Crossway)
I have said these things to you, that in Me you may have peace. In the world you will have tribulation. But take heart; I have overcome the world."

As I am wrapping up this chapter, I know I gave you a lot of information. I hope that the major takeaway is that the journey of faith is not an easy road, and every journey is different, but it's the greatest journey you could ever experience. God never promised us an easy road or experience, but He does promise that He will never leave us. I know as well as you, that there are a lot of hardships in this life. At times, it can feel like it takes every part of us just to make it through another day. But we have a light at the end of the tunnel, we have the hope of salvation and eternity with God, through Jesus. When the weight of this life is more than you can carry, God is there and God can handle the weight. He will be right there and will be the light to guide your way.

CHAPTER FIVE

WHAT ARE THE MARKS OF A CHRISTIAN?

Matthew 5:2-16 (English Standard Version (ESV)- 2001- Crossway)

And He opened His mouth and taught them, saying "Blessed are the poor in spirit, for theirs is the kingdom of Heaven. Blessed are those who mourn, for they shall be comforted. Blessed are the meek, for they shall inherit the Earth. Blessed are those who hunger and thirst for righteousness, for they shall be satisfied. Blessed are the merciful, for they shall receive mercy. Blessed are the pure in heart, for they shall see God. Blessed are the peacemakers, for they shall be called sons of God. Blessed are those who are persecuted for righteousness' sake, for theirs is the kingdom of Heaven. Blessed are you when others revile you and persecute you and utter all kinds of evil against you falsely on My account. Rejoice and be glad, for your reward is great in Heaven, for so they persecuted the prophets who were before you. You are the salt of the Earth, but if salt has lost its taste, how shall its saltiness be restored? It is no longer good for anything except to be thrown out and trampled under peoples feet. You are the light of the world. A city set on a hill cannot be hidden. Nor do people light a lamp and put it under a basket, but on a stand, and it gives light to all in the house. In the same way, let your light shine before others, so that they may see your good works and give glory to your Father who is in Heaven."

This was the beginning of one of the most popular sermons that Jesus gave during His time on Earth. There have been a lot of people who have written and preached about this sermon, which was called, 'The Sermon on the Mount.' There are plenty of people that have given a lot more intelligent feedback on this topic. I have never claimed to be a preacher, a theologian, or a Biblical scholar, but I think and hope the reason that you picked up this book is to hear from a normal, imperfect, everyday person that just has a heart for Christ and wants to share the love of God with others. When Jesus was about to give the most popular sermon of His time on Earth, I don't think a lot of people expected to hear, "Blessed are the poor in spirit." What does He even mean 'poor in spirit'? The first eleven verses of the sermon are called 'The Beatitudes', which I think you can say in simpler terms, that you are 'to be' or 'to have' these attitudes. Maybe I'm wrong, but I think it kind of works. A lot of these 'attitudes' that you are called to have, can seem kind of negative, such as poor in spirit, mourning, meek, hungry, thirsty, and persecuted. I don't know about you, but those don't sound super positive. So, what does being 'poor in spirit' mean? I believe it means that you should not be arrogant or self righteous. You are to keep in mind that you are a sinner in need of grace and God's love. You can't save yourself and you need to rely on God daily. Why are you blessed if you mourn? This is a lot like being poor in spirit, it is important to know the reverence and perfection of God and when we make life about us or choose to sin against our Creator, we become a part of driving a nail into the flesh of Jesus upon the Cross. We are to mourn and repent so that we can be forgiven. 'Blessed are the meek' also means to not be arrogant or self righteous, but to be kind and loving to others. Don't be so loud that you can't hear the needs of others. "Blessed are those who hunger and thirst for righteousness," as our bodies can't survive being malnourished, needing food and drink, we are to crave and strive for righteousness for the nourishment of our souls. Doing good for others feeds the spirit and leaves us fulfilled. Just as food and drink is essential to our bodies, our spirit is eternal and makes striving to do what is right far more necessary. They say giving is better than receiving, I believe that seeing the face of someone that you have served an act of kindness to, is beyond rewarding and vital for our souls. The next thing Jesus said was, "Blessed are the merciful," which means 'full of mercy,' showing kindness and love towards others. Mercy should be in the fiber of our being, even as we face death, we should show kindness and love. According to Oxford Languages on Google Dictionary, 'mercy', is defined as "compassion or forgiveness shown toward someone whom it is within one's power to punish or harm." Instead of casting judgment on someone, especially someone who might have done us wrong, we choose to show them kindness, love, and forgiveness. That is, in essence, what God showed to us. When we committed sin against Him, He still chose to give us His Son, who died for our sins. As a Christian, that is our number one job, to show kindness, forgiveness, and love, because that is what our God did for us. The next thing Jesus said is, "Blessed are the pure in heart, for they shall see God." This brings to question, what are your heart's desires and what are you feeding your heart? Are you being lustful, envious, greedy, or full of yourself? Are you looking at things you shouldn't, are you falling for an addiction? Is your whole life wrapped around how you can climb the corporate ladder for wealth and status? Your soul is being fed by your heart's desires. Are you feeding your soul things of sinful desires or are you feeding it God's word, love, forgiveness, hope, and grace. Is your soul focused on yourself or on God and others? When you seek your own desires, you will never achieve fulfillment; but when you seek to follow Christ, you inherit eternal life. The next thing Jesus says is, "Blessed are the peacemakers, for they shall be called sons of God." The first thing I want to say is that when it reads 'sons of God', I encourage you to read 'sons and daughters of God', or 'children of God.' When translating the Bible to English from the original language, some interpretations used the masculine pronouns generically. God loves all of us equally, we are all His children. Back to the point of this statement, where there is division and confrontation, we are called to show peace. We are not called to stir the pot, by adding to the drama of a family feud, or fueling divisions within political debates. We are to promote peace, truth, and love, being the truth tellers and not getting caught up in the pettiness.

The next couple of verses can pretty much be summed up in, "Blessed are those who are persecuted for righteousness' sake." The world did not take kindly to Jesus during His time on earth. From the beginning, Roman leadership wanted Him dead, so much so, that every male child under two years old was to be killed. Then, Jesus had religious leaders trying to find reasons to put Him to death, throughout His entire ministry. As they persecuted our Savior, we shall be persecuted as well. By being followers of Jesus, we will face persecution, but if we keep the faith, keep loving God, loving others, and then we become children of God. There are countries where Christians are killed just for being Christians. Here in America, we don't have that kind of persecution, but we are persecuted in other ways. We can be ridiculed for believing in a higher power or for not being open to other theologies. Unfortunately, I have experienced the most judgment from within the people of the Christian faith. They judge if you don't believe or belong to their church denomination, or if you have a different theology. There is a vast division of theological beliefs between the Arminian and Calvinist doctrines. The theological division centers around whether you have a free will or if everything has been predestined. There is division about baby baptism versus adult baptism. There are too many divisions that are making faith more about religion, rather than focusing on God, His love and grace, and about the greatest commandment. Sometimes it's hard to believe that so many people claim to follow Jesus, but are still involved with the religious system, the very one that Jesus fought so hard against. It makes me wonder if these Christians today truly grasp Jesus' intense words against the Pharisees and Sadducees, the religious leaders, who valued tradition over the welfare of the people. For example, Jesus performed multiple healings on the Sabbath, the day of rest, which upset the religious leaders, due to the fact that that action was in opposition of the law. Going back to the Bible scripture, "Blessed are those who are persecuted for righteousness' sake", as our Savior was persecuted, we are not promised an easy journey. In fact, we are promised persecution because of our faith, but we have an eternal hope of salvation in Christ.

The next topic that Jesus talked about was salt and light. Salt was very important in Biblical times due to no refrigeration and for seasoning food. As salt preserves and seasons food, we are to preserve the Word of God in our hearts and share it with others. Likewise, we are to be the light of God to the world. We need light to see through the darkness, and we need to share that light in the world of darkness. We need people to see the goodness and the love of Christ through our good works. We don't need people to see our good works, so that we can be recognized and praised, but that those good works point them to Jesus, the light of the world.

Matthew 16:24-26 (English Standard Version (ESV)- 2001- Crossway)
Then Jesus told His disciples, "If anyone would come after Me, let him deny himself and take up his cross and follow Me. For whoever would save his life will lose it, but whoever loses his life for My sake will find it. For what will it profit a man if he gains the whole world and forfeits his soul?

Ephesians 4:1-3 (English Standard Version (ESV)- 2001- Crossway)
I therefore, a prisoner for the Lord, urge you to walk in a manner worthy of the calling to which you have been called, with all humility and gentleness, with patience, bearing with one another, eager to maintain the unity of the Spirit in the bond of peace.

Philippians 1:21 (English Standard Version (ESV)- 2001- Crossway)
For me to live is Christ, and to die is gain.

I titled this book 'Saving Grace- It's Not About You Anymore.' I think these verses really pack a punch with that point. We are not to value this life as if this is all there is. I have heard this analogy that I really like- this life is just a test before eternity. We struggle now with blind faith, but after this life we won't need faith, we won't need prayer, we will be with God. This life is focused on fighting our sinful desires, praying for souls, resisting evil, and showing love. Jesus asks us to pick up our cross, which is a symbol of death, and follow Him. The Apostle Paul wrote the majority of the New Testament while in prison. He was persecuted for the sake of Christ. He got to the point where he was ready to leave this life to be with Jesus, but he knew that there was more work to be done.

He truly knew that the meaning of this life was to spread the Gospel. Knowing this, what is a mark of a Christian? It is knowing that this life is temporary and that our mission while here, is to love God, love others, and share the good news of Jesus.

I know that a lot of this chapter might feel pretty heavy and depressing. It might even seem like there can be no joy as a Christian. I promise that isn't true. I often think about how big and beautiful God's creation is and all of the places that you can see and travel to. I remember gazing at a sunset from a beach in Puerto Rico, and it really made me pause in awe of the majesty of God. There are places that I would love to go see in person. For example, I would love to go see the Holy Land, where they guide you through all of the places that Jesus walked. I would love to see Mt. Everest, the scenery of the 'Lord Of The Rings' films, the pyramids of Egypt, and all of the wonders of the world. There are times that I really think that it's unfair that we live in a culture where we need to work the majority of our lives to get by, when there is a whole world to see. I more than likely will never make it to those places in my lifetime, but that doesn't mean that I don't have joy in my life. Do you know where I find my joy? It doesn't have to be extravagant. I love having a couple of drinks with my girlfriend around a bonfire, and watching movies with her. I love spending time and having real-life talks with my friends, where people are open and honest with each other. I enjoy looking up to the stars on a perfect summer night, and falling asleep next to the person I love. Having the right people in your life is so important. Someone you can laugh with and someone you can lean on, and them knowing that they can lean on you. There is always joy and blessings in the little moments. God did a good job with creating people!

As I wrap up this chapter, I want you to remember that God does ask hard things of us. He truly asks that we give up our old ways, our desires, and to follow Him. He does not promise an easy road, but the journey with God is more rewarding than we could ever know. When Jesus called His disciples, they literally left everything behind. They left their homes, their families, their careers, and their way of life. They traveled on foot, from town to town, learning from Jesus, witnessing miracles, listening to Jesus preach, and were able to be a part of His ministry. I'm sure there were some really difficult times, but the journey was incredible. Their life, from the moment they decided to follow Jesus, was Jesus. They made their mistakes, they didn't understand everything, but they had commitment and they had faith. I believe that is what Jesus is asking of us. We need to be willing to leave our old ways behind, give Him our commitment and faith, and just be willing to start this wild ride. We won't be perfect, we won't always understand, but we are a part of something bigger than ourselves. It will truly be a wild ride!

CHAPTER SIX

RICHES DON'T EQUAL WEALTH

Matthew 19:16-30 (English Standard Version (ESV)- 2001- Crossway)

And behold, a man came up to Him, saying, "Teacher, what good deed must I do to have eternal life?" And He said to him, "Why do you ask Me about what is good? There is only One who is good. If you would enter life, keep the commandments." He said to Him, "Which ones?" And Jesus said, "You shall not murder, you shall not commit adultery, you shall not steal, you shall not bear false witness, honor your father and mother, and, you shall love your neighbor as yourself." The young man said to Him, "All these I have kept. What do I still lack?" Jesus said to him, "If you would be perfect, go, sell what you possess and give to the poor, and you will have treasure in Heaven; and come, follow Me." When the young man heard this he went away sorrowful, for he had great possessions. And Jesus said to His disciples, "Truly, I say to you, only with difficulty will a rich person enter the kingdom of Heaven. Again I tell you, it is easier for a camel to go through the eye of a needle than for a rich person to enter the kingdom of God." When the disciples heard this, they were greatly astonished, saying, "Who then can be saved?" But Jesus looked at them and said, "With man this is impossible, but with God all things are possible." Then Peter said in reply, "See, we have left everything and followed You. What then will we have?" Jesus said to them, "Truly, I say to you, in the new world, when the Son of Man will sit on His glorious throne, you who have followed Me will also sit on twelve thrones, judging the twelve tribes of Israel. And everyone who has left houses or brothers or sisters or father or mother or children or lands, for My name's sake, will receive a hundredfold and will inherit eternal life. But many who are first will be last, and the last first.

I want you to envision a successful guy. He has always been 'well-liked', so much so, that he was the Prom King at his high school. He was always under pressure from his parents to perform his best. He was the starting

Quarterback on his high school football team, and continued to play in college. He graduated with a Master's degree in business, with honors. He married the Prom Queen from high school. He bought a nice house, was a father of three children, and was just promoted to the top position at his firm. Every day, he walked past a homeless beggar on the way to his office. The beggar held a sign that said, "I once was blind, but now I see, would you please help me?" The beggar was a blind man, but had such a remarkable smile, that the guy couldn't help but notice it. Still, he walked by the beggar every day. One Friday night, the guy met up with his co-workers at a local bar to celebrate a successful business deal, drinking to the point of being intoxicated. While at the bar, the guy noticed that he had forgotten something from work, so he drove to his office. As he drove, he noticed a huge bump in the road. He then realized that he had just run over the beggar that he passed every day on his way to work. The beggar didn't survive. The cops came and arrested the guy that night. The guy was locked up with nothing but his guilt and his thoughts. The next day, the guy had a surprise visitor. It was a female, that he later found out, was the beggar's daughter. She was in tears and she couldn't speak, but she handed him a note and then ran out. The guy opened the note and it read, "God still loves you, come back to Him."

He dropped the note and broke into tears. He thought that he had it all, the house, the wife, the children, the job, but with the silence of the jail cell, he was left so empty. He had taken everything for granted, and somehow this blind beggar had had it all, because he had God.

Going back to the set of verses, the rich man had everything, or so he thought. He thought he was a moral and upright citizen. He couldn't imagine that he wasn't good enough for eternal life. I'm sure that he was raised in church, went to Bible studies, and felt like he was good enough. Jesus questioned the rich man, asking how could he even assume that he knows what is good, only God is good. When the rich man said that he hadn't committed murder, adultery, theft, bore false witness (he hadn't lied), honored his parents, and loved his neighbors as himself, Jesus knew his heart. Going back to Jesus' sermon, the 'Sermon on the Mount', Jesus went deeper into the heart of the commandments. I will share a few examples.

Matthew 5:21-22 (English Standard Version (ESV)- 2001- Crossway)
"You have heard that it was said to those of old, 'You shall not murder; and whoever murders will be liable to judgment. But I say to you that everyone who is angry with his brother will be liable to judgment; whoever

insults his brother will be liable to council; and whoever says, 'You fool!' will be liable to the hell of fire."

Matthew 5:27-28 (English Standard Version (ESV)- 2001- Crossway)
"You have heard that it was said, 'You shall not commit adultery.' But I say to you that everyone who looks at a woman with lustful intent has already committed adultery with her in his heart."

Matthew 5:38-42 (English Standard Version (ESV)- 2001- Crossway)
"You have heard it was said, 'An eye for an eye and a tooth for a tooth.' But I say to you, do not resist the one who is evil. But if anyone slaps you on the right cheek, turn to him the other also. And if anyone would sue you and take your tunic, let him have your cloak as well. And if anyone forces you to go one mile, go with him two miles. Give to the one who begs from you, and do not refuse the one who would borrow from you."

Matthew 5:43-44 (English Standard Version (ESV)- 2001- Crossway)
"You have heard that it was said, 'You shall love your neighbor and hate your enemy.' But I say to you, 'Love your enemies and pray for those who persecute you.'"

What Jesus is saying with these verses is that it's not good enough to just not kill someone, but you are not to even be angry with someone. Not only are you not to cheat on your spouse, but don't even let your eyes wander to anyone else. Don't feel justified in repaying wrongdoing with wrongdoing, but go above and beyond by showing the wrongdoer love and grace. When Jesus said that only One is good, that is because we fall so short in keeping the heart of the commandments. It is probably easy for most of us to not get a gun out and shoot someone, but to not even be angry with someone that has done us wrong is very, very hard. That is why we need God's grace. We can never fully measure up.

After the rich man tries to tell Jesus that he has kept the commandments, Jesus then points to the rich man's greatest selfish desire, his wealth and possessions. If the rich man could give up his wealth and possessions to follow Jesus, that would truly be a sign of repentance, faith, and love. But because the rich man's first love was his wealth and possessions, he was not willing to give them away to follow Jesus. That is where he really messed up. He was provided the way of salvation, but he chose his desires. His wealth would eventually make him the poorest of the poor. I find it very interesting, and almost amusing, that the disciples were astonished when Jesus said that it is almost impossible for the rich to be saved. I've always loved the analogy of trying to picture a camel going through the eye of a needle. I think Jesus had a great sense of humor. In church, religion, and even society, I think it's very easy to believe that the rich, powerful, and important people are definitely on the right path. There's no way the President of the United States could go to hell, right? If not them, how could an ordinary and insignificant me be worthy of God? God honors humility and opposes the proud. God looks at the heart. The more we give of ourselves in this life, the higher the reward we will have in Heaven. The more we focus on ourselves, the less we will be rewarded.

Imagine a cross-country race. All of the crowd is cheering on the top two competitors amongst all of the top runners of their state. When the race starts, both competitors give it their all, but they witness one of the other runners trip on a rock, fall, and break their leg. One of the top two competitors ran right past the injured runner, to make sure that he wins the race, the other top competitor stopped and asked if the injured runner was alright. He lifted up the injured runner and took him to the medical team. The top competitor who ran past the injured runner won the race, but to his surprise there was no cheering, or clapping, instead, the competitor who left the race to help the injured runner received all of the cheers and was covered in the news articles about the race. It wasn't about the winner, but it was about the competitor who showed compassion. Jesus couldn't care less about who had won the race, but His eyes are focused on those who help the one in need.

Matthew 20:1-16 (English Standard Version (ESV)- 2001- Crossway)
"For the kingdom of Heaven is like a master of a house who went out early in the morning to hire laborers for his vineyard. After agreeing with the laborers for a denarius a day, he sent them into his vineyard. And going out about the third hour he saw others standing idle in the marketplace, and to them he said, 'You go into the vineyard too, and whatever is right I will give you.' So they went. Going out again about the sixth hour and the ninth hour, he did the same. And about the eleventh hour he went out and found others standing. And he said to them, 'Why do you stand here idle all day?' They said to him, 'Because no one has hired us.' He said to them, 'You go into the vineyard too.' And when evening came, the owner of the vineyard said to his foreman, 'Call the laborers and pay them their wages, beginning with the last, up to the first.' And when those hired about the eleventh hour came, each of them received a denarius. Now when those hired first

came, they thought they would receive more, but each of them also received a denarius. And on receiving it they grumbled at the master of the house, saying, "These last worked only one hour, and you have made them equal to us who have borne the burden of the day and the scorching heat.' But he replied to one of them, 'Friend, I am doing you no wrong. Did you not agree with me for a denarius? Take what belongs to you and go. I choose to give this last worker as I give to you. Am I not allowed to do what I choose with what belongs to me? Or do you begrudge my generosity?' So the last will be first, and the first last."

The parable of Jesus, or story that Jesus told, can be a very tough pill to swallow, but it can be the most freeing. In this story, Jesus is comparing a worker in the vineyard to a person following Jesus. The people, who were hired first in the vineyard, had to work the longest in very hard conditions, just as people who have followed Jesus for their whole lives, had to struggle with the battle of sin and the hardships of following Christ. The workers that were first hired in the vineyard, were able to work the whole day and made their agreed upon wage, when obviously a lot of others were not getting hired that day. Even though they had a long work day, they were prepared for it, because that was what they agreed to. What they were frustrated with was that the owner of the vineyard had hired other workers who worked less and got the same payment. It is not hard to understand why the workers, who started at the beginning of the day, would be frustrated. Logic says that the more you work, the more you earn. The harder you try, the more you deserve. Place yourself in the mindset of the workers who were hired last. They waited around all day hoping to get hired and make a wage to survive. They probably watched worker after worker getting hired, while they are left another day with no way to make a wage, to pay their bills or feed their family. After hours went by, I'm sure they were discouraged. Then at the eleventh hour of the work day, a vineyard owner actually acknowledges them. They probably went in thinking that maybe they'd get a percentage of the day's wage that would be better than nothing. Then again, think about what receiving the full amount of a work day meant to them. I'm sure they were speechless. After so much discouragement, they received an underserved gift, also known as grace. You can bet that they valued every bite of their next meal, like every bite was the best bite that they had tasted in their whole life. If you bring this concept to today, there are so many people who work their whole lives to achieve 'The American

Dream.' They go to college to have a high paying career, get married, buy a nice house, have kids, a nice car, go on vacations, and get set up to have a perfect retirement. They live their whole life in hope of having a 'light at the end of the tunnel', which in this case means having a great retirement. Their focus is often too narrow to see the bigger picture. Sadly, they go down the path that has the same destination as everyone else born on earth, which is death. They do so much to make a great life on this earth, but they lose sight of what is really important. In the end, they will be judged the same as everyone else. It doesn't matter how big of a house you have, or what you have in your bank account. What matters is how much you have loved others.

One of my all time favorite stories is Charles Dickens', 'A Christmas Carol.' I own many different versions of the movie based on this story. I'm sure that you are familiar with the story so I won't go too deep into the storyline, but I will address a few topics. Ebenezer Scrooge is a mean and cold-hearted man that hates the world and everyone in it. His only love is his massive fortune. He has more money than you can dream of and he lives more frugally than a poor person, so that he does not waste his fortune. He gets haunted by three Christmas ghosts. One ghost, representing Christmas past, shared with him memories from his past, how he had been hurt by people in his life, and had chosen a life of greed rather than love. Then, the second ghost was the ghost of Christmas present, which showed him the pain and misfortune of the people in Scrooge's life that he overlooks, because all he cares about is his wealth. Lastly, the third ghost is the ghost of Christmas yet to come, which shows him the horrible futures of the people in his life who have been damned to a life of pain and misfortune, stemming from poverty, and the ghost shows him what would happen to Scrooge himself if nothing changes. This experience really woke Ebenezer Scrooge up and shook him to his core. Being the wealthiest person truly made him the poorest of the poor. The life that he was living, not only harmed the people around him, but was also damning him to a future of eternal punishment. What you do in this life doesn't only affect your life, but also affects others around you, and the only true wealth is found in love.

Matthew 6:25-34 (English Standard Version (ESV)- 2001- Crossway)
"Therefore I tell you, do not be anxious about your life, what you will eat or what you will drink, nor about your body, what you will put on. Is not life more than food, and the body more than clothing? Look at the birds of the air:

they neither sow nor reap nor gather into barns, and yet your Heavenly Father feeds them. Are you not of more value than they? And which of you by being anxious can add a single hour to his span of life? And why are you anxious about clothing? Consider the lilies of the field, how they grow: they neither toil nor spin, yet I tell you, even Solomon in all his glory was not arrayed like one of these. But if God so clothes the grass of the field, which today is alive and tomorrow is thrown into the oven, will He not much more clothe you, O you of little faith? Therefore do not be anxious, saying, 'What shall we eat?' or 'What shall we drink?' or 'What shall we wear?' For the Gentiles seek after all these things, and your Heavenly Father knows that you need them all. But seek first the kingdom of God and His righteousness, and all these things will be added to you. Therefore do not be anxious about tomorrow, for tomorrow will be anxious for itself. Sufficient for the day is its own trouble."

The society we live in is very money-driven. Everything costs money and it's not cheap either. Money is a pretty uncomfortable topic. Reading Bible verses about being rich and greedy can seem like a one-way ticket to hell. It can seem pretty intense when not having enough money feels like a struggle to get by. Especially with the political climate, the war of Russia and Ukraine, rising gas prices, the COVID-19 pandemic, having some money doesn't seem like a bad idea. It's very easy to get anxious about finances. It feels like we have to work so much just to get by. I have a few things that I want to share with you concerning money. First of all, money isn't evil, the love of money is. It's not wrong to be fiscally responsible, because the fact of the matter is that we need to make an income to survive. We need a roof over our head, we need food and drink, we need gas in our car. We can't get these things without money. What is wrong is when we let money control our lives and let the love of money control our hearts. If we care more about finances to put an addition on our house instead of helping our neighbor in need, is where we come to a problem. If we care more about upgrading to a better and more expensive car, when we see someone struggling with getting their basic needs met, we are putting our sinful desires ahead of loving our neighbor. That is where we cross a line.

I also know that it is easy to be overcome by giving up our passions and love, because it's thought not to be fiscally responsible. We get caught up with having to work jobs that we don't like, because we need to make that next paycheck. Like I said, we do need money to live, we are not supposed to be irresponsible, but we are also supposed to have faith in God. We are not supposed to always have an anxiety attack, because things are tough. God knows us and loves us deeply. He wants us to trust, rely on Him, and He promises to meet our needs. Instead of worrying so much about the next paycheck, we should be asking ourselves how to put more trust in God. We should be asking ourselves if we are loving God and our neighbor. Am I letting go of my desires and following Jesus today?

I have always had a passion for music and writing. I never really knew what I wanted to do for a career. I just knew that I had a heart for people. In my heart of hearts, I knew that I wanted to impact people for Christ with my writing. Let me tell you something, writing does not pay the bills. I believe that I have the gift of writing, which helps my personal faith, my relationship with God, and I know this is something that I need to pursue. It's a place where I know that I'm seeking the kingdom of God. It gets me to a place where I'm reading, digging into the word of God, and it's a place where it's a type of prayer for me. Pursuing writing has cost me a lot of time and money, but I know that I can't give up on it, and it really does fulfill me spiritually. I also have taken a leap of faith in my work life. I had a steady job with a steady income, working with great people, but it was affecting my home life. My girlfriend and I have been having a tough time because our lives have been so focused on work and not our relationship. I took a leap of faith to start a residential cleaning company, using the knowledge that I had gained, and using my strong work ethic. A lot of people have said that it wasn't the smartest financial decision, but I am relying on what the word of God says. As I seek God first, He promises to meet my needs. He doesn't promise to keep us on the easy road. I ask that He use my life in this next adventure as I continue seeking Him. I have no desire to be the richest person, I want to go on the wild adventure of giving my everything and follow Jesus. I want to be done with being just a fisher of fish and go on to become a fisher of men. I pray that you know that riches don't equal wealth. I pray that you know that true wealth is a life of following Jesus.

CHAPTER SEVEN

HUMILITY OVER GREATNESS

Matthew 18:1-4 (English Standard Version (ESV)- 2001- Crossway)

At that time the disciples came to Jesus, saying, "Who is the greatest in the kingdom of Heaven?" And calling to Him a child, He put him in the midst of them and said, "Truly, I say to you, unless you turn and become like children, you will never enter the kingdom of Heaven. Whoever humbles himself like this child is the greatest in the kingdom of Heaven."

Children are definitely gifts from God. They are loving, innocent, and vulnerable. They rely on the love of others. They haven't been corrupted by pride. We are called to rely on the love of God and be humble enough to know our need for Him. In this world, so many people believe life is some competition and they have to be better than everyone else. I believe it's human nature to want to be the best. Like I said towards the beginning of the book, I believe the root of all sin is rooted in selfishness. People want to be the greatest and they want to feel like they deserve it all. What they are really doing is digging themselves deeper into the grave. Like I have said in this book multiple times, people want to chase the 'American Dream'. They want a successful career, they want an amazing marriage, they want a beautiful house, they want children, they want amazing vacations, they want all of the luxuries of life, and they want to retire with all the benefits. They also want to push their children to be great and want them to know how important it is to succeed, and they want to make sure they have grandchildren to maintain their family name and legacy. These people will often go to church on Sundays, so that they maintain their appearance as being good and Godly people. Unfortunately, people living this lifestyle have missed the point. I know that the 'American Dream' mentality is really pushed in an unconscious way in our culture. People in society may not even consciously know that they are doing it, but it is rooted in their sinful nature. You can see it in their politics, in the busyness of their life, in the way they are looking at their phones, rather than each other. The parents need to keep climbing the corporate ladder, make the next business deal, go home, and get their kids ready for sports, in order to win that next game. The parents then push the kids to earn that scholarship to a great college, so that they can start a family with children who will do the same. Our culture needs to slow down. We need to stop worrying about being successful and take a moment to be kind. Our culture needs to stop being so competitive and be more compassionate. We need to stop worrying about what the President is doing and start thinking about what we are doing. Stop waiting for someone else to help our neighbor, when we are right there. We need to stop pointing the finger and start looking in the mirror. I want to make sure that I say that there is nothing wrong with having a good job, being a homeowner, having a family, wanting your children to succeed, but the focus shouldn't be prideful or with selfish intent. We should work hard, we should love our families, and want what is best for our loved ones. There is a point where we need to make sure we ask ourselves if we are loving God with everything that we are doing, and are we loving our neighbor? Are we trying to get the best of everything for our luxury, or are we blessing people? Are we relying on God, or are we relying on ourselves? Are we keeping the heart of a child, or are we driven by selfish ambition?

One of my best friends in this world is a guy named Eric. We met at a local church, where he was playing in the worship band. The church service and sermon were about losing someone to suicide and I broke down. I had lost a great friend named Caleb to suicide, during a really hard time in my life, and it deeply affected me. After the sermon, during the last song of the church service, I was crying, Eric came to me afterwards, and prayed with me. We then started getting lunch together biweekly. He became a Christian mentor of mine. At one point, when our daily lives were getting too busy, I asked him if he liked beer. I was hesitant when asking, because he was a member of the church band and a dad, but he said, "Are you kidding me, of course I do, haha." We were able to go to the local bar every other week, had some food, a couple of beers, and our friendship really grew. When I started dating my girlfriend, I really wanted him to meet her and befriend her, because after her divorce she really didn't have anyone besides myself and our friend, Big Mike, who is like a brother to us. I was nervous, because Debby's and my relationship is untraditional due to an age difference, and I was concerned that he wouldn't appreciate it and would judge us. Eric welcomed Debby with open arms and he truly sees the love that we have for each other. Our biweekly hangouts mean the world to us. He truly shows us the love of Christ. He is a busy business owner, husband, and father, but he deliberately and intentionally makes an effort to have our evening hangouts work. We talk about life, how each of us is doing, and just share life with each other. We have asked him to lead our future commitment ceremony, that is dedicating our relationship to God. Eric and his family are such a blessing and they truly have a heart for people. They are busy with all of the traditional family stuff, jobs, raising kids, angsty teenagers, taking them to sporting events, and everything home life requires, but they still make it a priority to make time for people. I admire that so much. Eric loves like Jesus and never judges. He will let me know if he disagrees with something, or let me know when I'm being an idiot, but he will also encourage me and support me. He is truly a brother in Christ. I am so blessed and honored that Eric is willing to lead our commitment ceremony when we dedicate our relationship to God. Debby and I are so grateful for his love and his support. We get to be real, shed some tears, but more often than not, just have some drinks, laugh, and enjoy each other's company.

Do nothing from rivalry or conceit, but in humility count others more significant than yourselves. Let each of you look not only to his own interests, but also the interests of others. Have this mind among yourselves, which is yours in Christ Jesus, who, though He was in the form of God, did not count equality with God a thing to be grasped, but made Himself nothing, taking the form of a servant, being born in the likeness of men. And being found in human form, He humbled Himself by becoming obedient to the point of death, even death on a cross.

We have all seen war movies that captivate us, make us wish we could be there, and fight for the cause. We see these characters fight, give their lives for their cause, and for their fellow warriors. We all want to be a part of something greater than ourselves. Jesus, our Savior, the one true Son of God, came down from His throne to die for us, so that we could spend eternity with Him in Paradise. He gave up everything to be a child of very humble parents, who did not have much to give, but their faith and trust. They were willing to give up everything, even their reputation, to be servants of God. I'm sure you have heard of Jesus' mother, the Virgin Mary. It is easy to think of her as a significant and important religious figure.

The Catholic churches have beautiful portraits of Mary and even pray to her. In reality, she was a simple and poor girl. Her family needed her to marry, so that they could assure their future. She then learned from an angel that she was going to conceive Jesus, the Son of God, the Savior that was foretold. The catch was, she was going to conceive while still being a virgin. I don't know about you, but that is scientifically impossible and it isn't going to help her reputation. God didn't choose Mary because of her status or importance, but because she was humble and faithful. She had the heart of a servant, as well as her husband-to-be, Joseph. He was not a man of great significance either. He was a young man who was a common worker with a good heart. Obviously, when he was informed that his bride-to-be was with child and he had never been "with" her, that must have felt like betrayal. He must have been very hurt and felt that all trust was broken. Instead of following the law, which gave him the right to stone Mary, he put his pride aside, put Mary above his own feelings, and decided to leave her quietly. Even before an angel came to Joseph confirming all that Mary had said, Joseph showed love and humility, and afterwards, he believed the angel wholeheartedly. Regardless of his reputation, Joseph was going to be there and love his bride-to-be. He had the heart of a servant, putting others before himself. Joseph was not mentioned extensively in the Bible. The most common belief was that he died before Jesus' ministry began. Joseph was an incredible character in the Bible, not because he was powerful or well-to-do, but because he had a servant's heart full of humility, faith, and love. We, as people, want to be important and be remembered. We search for our "15 minutes of fame." We see celebrities on TV, probably viewed more often nowadays on our phones, and we want to be as famous and important as them. In reality, celebrities are probably the least happy of people. They have the wealth and fame, but they experience many divorces, addictions, and spend their whole lives entertaining others. Oftentimes, neglecting their own spiritual well-being, celebrities always need to be in the spotlight or they are soon forgotten. That lifestyle does not bring fulfillment, whereas our true purpose is found in Jesus. Serving God, loving others, living for something much greater than ourselves is where we find true worth.

Romans 12:16 (English Standard Version (ESV)- 2001- Crossway)
Live in harmony with one another. Do not be haughty, but associate with the lowly. Never be wise in your own sight.

The definition of 'haughty', according to Oxford Language

on Google Dictionary is, "arrogantly superior and disdainful." We are called to not think of ourselves as more important or wise than anyone else. As Jesus was our example, we are called to hang-out and surround ourselves with the marginalized and the outcasts. We are called to meet them where they are and to be there with them.

Consider a small town church community. A community where everyone knows everyone else. They gather together every Sunday to enjoy a great sermon, worship music, fellowship to encourage one another, and to enjoy a meal together. Oftentimes, they will do community outreaches that include banquets to help feed the homeless, visit nursing homes, and things of that nature. One member of the worship band, who is just about to graduate from high school, has been questioning himself, and being questioned by others, about what it is that he wants to do with his life. His family has been going to that church since before he was born, and this community is all that he has ever known. He has heard sermons and has read his Bible about the importance of showing Christ's love and serving others. He has an internal conflict within himself, because he loves the people in his community, but he also believes that his faith is not being challenged. He is at a place in his life where he feels that he is in a spiritually safe place, but he has this feeling in his gut that he needs to be more radical with serving and loving others. He has met with the pastor of the church about his internal conflict and the pastor's recommendation made him feel underwhelmed. His pastor told him, "You can serve people where you are, you can go to college, learn more about God, and build your future, so that you can grow and love others." Everyone has been telling him to go to college and grow, while he has been dreaming about moving to Africa and serving amongst tribes that live in severe poverty, with none of the comforts of his home. He eventually decides that he needs to go where he feels God is calling him to go. After graduation, he acquires everything needed for the life changing move to Africa. He said his goodbyes to his family and to his small town community. He arrives at an African community where famine and disease run rampant. He saw the love and strength of the people. He thought that he was moving there to help them, but in reality he was humbled and he learned from them. He saw the reliance they had on God and for each other. They had next to no possessions and still they wanted for not. Every day was a struggle, every day they had to rely on God, and every day they had to rely on each other. Every person in that community had more faith than any individual he had met in his small town community. No person thought that they were more important than anyone else. There was no competition, there was only compassion. There was no judgment, only kindness. There was no pridefulness, only reliance. There was no hate, only mercy and grace. He remained in Africa for the rest of his days. He may have never enjoyed the riches of the American culture, but he lived knowing the wealth that is in God and the value of loving others. He was humbled and had gained more reward than he had ever thought possible.

As I wrap up this chapter, it is so much more important to be humble than to be prideful. We are called to be meek, not to be great. We are to be compassionate, rather than competitive. We are not to judge, but to give grace. Remember, that there is nothing that we can do to earn salvation. We are saved by the free gift of grace. Our number one goal in this life is to love God and love others.

CHAPTER EIGHT

JUDGE AND YOU WILL BE JUDGED

Matthew 7:1-5 (English Standard Version (ESV)- 2001- Crossway)
"Judge not, that you be not judged. For with the judgment you pronounce you will be judged, and with the measure you use it will be measured to you. Why do you see the speck that is in your brother's eye, but do not notice the log that is in your own eye? You hypocrite, first take the log out of your own eye, then you will see clearly the speck out of your brother's eye."

There is an amazing Christian community called, 'The Happy Givers', that is a ministry founded by Carlos A. Rodriquez, based in Puerto Rico. They are aggressively passionate about loving the marginalized. Their main mission is to live by the Bible verses Matthew 25:35-46.

Matthew 25:35-46 (English Standard Version (ESV)- 2001- Crossway)

"For I was hungry and you gave Me food, I was thirsty and you gave Me drink, I was a stranger and you welcomed Me, I was naked and you clothed Me, I was sick and you visited Me, I was in prison and you came to Me.' Then the righteous will answer Him, saying, "Lord, when did we see You hungry and feed You, or thirsty and give You drink? And when did we see You sick or in prison and visit You?' And the King will answer them, 'Truly, I say to you, as you did it to one of the least of these my brothers, you did it to Me.' "Then He will say to those on His left, 'Depart from Me, you cursed, into the eternal fire prepared for the Devil and his angels. For I was hungry and you gave Me no food, I was thirsty and you gave Me no drink, I was a stranger and you did not welcome Me, naked and you did not clothe Me, sick and in prison and you did not visit Me.' Then they also will answer, saying, 'Lord, when did we see You hungry or thirsty or a stranger or naked or sick or in prison, and did not minister to You?' Then He will answer them, saying, 'Truly, I say to you, as you did not do it to one of the least of these, you did not do it to Me.' And these will go away into the eternal punishment, but the righteous into eternal life."

I mentioned these verses in the beginning of chapter 3. These verses are saying that if you ignore the hungry, thirsty, stranger, naked, sick, and imprisoned then you ignore Jesus, but if you welcome and love them, you do that also to Jesus. I bought two sweatshirts from 'The Happy Givers Ministry' that I have really loved. The first one says, "If you hate anyone because of your faith, you're doing it wrong." The second one says, "Jesus is the refugee, the man on death row, the child at the border, the single mom with two jobs, the person with a disability, the friend with an addiction, the transgender co-worker, the kid with no lunch money. How you treat them is how you treat Jesus." I think that sweatshirt really personifies and personalizes what Jesus is saying in Matthew 25:35-46. Today's culture judges or hates these people at the worst, or at best, just overlooks them. How often do you take the time to engage with the marginalized? Not just acknowledge that they exist, but take time to listen to them and hear their story. The 'America first' philosophy divides us into seeing refugees as political pawns rather than real people with needs. It is said that refugees could possibly be radical Muslims, or have the intent to destroy the American culture, instead of just seeing them as God's children, people that are loved, but in need. When we think about a man on death row, it's easy to first think that the guy must have done something really messed up to be on death row, he is obviously an evil person. In reality, we are all sinners and we all don't deserve grace. We have all fallen short of God's law. This brings me back to thinking about a lyric from one of my favorite bands, 'August Burns Red'. The song is titled, 'Provision', which includes the lyrics: "I'm just as much the problem as the man behind bars. He did with his business what I do in my heart." We are all sinners, just because we didn't do something that puts us in prison, doesn't mean the person in prison, or even the one on death row, deserves any less love than us. When we think of a single mom with two kids, are we judging her as a promiscuous person, or are we seeing her as someone who has a past, but is striving to be enough. When we see someone with a disability, it is easy to overlook them, because they make us uncomfortable. As I talked about in chapter 3, people with disabilities, such as Down syndrome, are beautiful souls, but it takes time and effort to build a relationship with them. They have desires and goals, like all of us do, and they don't want to be treated any differently. So many of us push the disabled to the side, because they are different and it can be awkward. We are called to show them love, take the time and effort to get to know them. They are such a blessing and are worthy of love. When we hear about people with an addiction, especially a drug addiction, it is all too common to judge them. How low could they be to do hard drugs like cocaine, meth, or any other drug? It is easy to see them as losers or criminals. These people are broken and in need of love and support. A life of addiction starts with one mistake and it is a slippery slope to being controlled by a substance. They are in need of love, support, and grace like the rest of us. People in the LGBTQ community are often judged, especially by the Christian community. They think the lifestyle is not natural and it's a sin. They want to protest against gay marriage and push for traditional marriage, instead of getting to know people and listen to them. They want to fight against transgender rights, while wanting nothing to do with the transgender community. It is a lot easier to hate someone that you don't know. It's harder to hate someone you have met and spent time with. I have heard stories of how guys felt pushed away from churches, because they are gay and they are told that it is a sin which will send them to hell. That is not love. People in the LGBTQ community deserve God's love and grace just like everyone else. People also judge those who are poor. They think that people in poverty are just lazy and live off of the government. These kids who don't have enough lunch money must have "bum" parents who don't support them. People question why their tax dollars are used to help people who don't help themselves. People make a lot of assumptions while closing their eyes to the struggles of poverty. There are families that have to work multiple jobs just to be able to afford basic necessities, such as housing and food. A lot of people don't know what it's like to be caught up in the government system, or what it's like to struggle to survive. Those in poverty deserve love, support, people believing in them, mercy, and grace. I have a heart for the outcasts and marginalized, not only because that is what is commanded of us biblically, but because of the struggles of my past and the examples of the people who are in my life. People who are pushed aside, because they are different, are oftentimes the people with the most love and beautifulest of souls. The less we have, the more grateful we are for what we do have. If you are loved by everyone in the community, the easier it is to take love for granted. If you are loved by just a few people, you know the value of those relationships. The more you value the relationship, the more you will fight for it. If you have a house full of everything you need, then the more you take for granted, and the less you appreciate the little things. Having less tends to make you more grateful for the little things.

Imagine two middle school boys. One boy has the best of everything. He has exclusively name brand clothes, he owns the top-notch video gaming systems, and every game that you can imagine. Every person in his class wants to be his friend. This middle school boy makes high schoolers jealous, because his parents have a Ford Mustang just waiting for him when he gets his driver's license. For Christmas, he was promised that he would get the newest video gaming system, six months before it gets released to the public. When Christmas came and he didn't get it, the boy threw a fit, smashed all of his video gaming systems against the wall, and screamed, "Get it now!" The parents made calls and corrupted deals with the game designers to get their son that video gaming system. Now, the other boy lives in a low-income apartment with his single mother, who works three jobs to make ends meet. The best meal of his day is the school lunch that he receives on the free/reduced lunch program. Even this meal he often misses, because it gets destroyed by the bullies who pick on him. He owns a couple of pairs of blue jeans, a few t-shirts, and his favorite black hooded sweatshirt. He sometimes gets to see his mom before school and he often hears her coming into their apartment in the early morning hours, after her last job. His favorite pastime is drawing pictures of his favorite video game hero that he only gets to see in commercials. He has never had the opportunity to have his own video gaming system, but he has a memory of playing his father's system on the

TV, in the living room, when he was young. As he would try to focus on the game, he would hear his drunk father beating on his mom. After his father passed out in bed, his mother quietly grabbed their things and took him away from playing the video game, never seeing his father again. As he did that night, he desperately wanted to be that hero from that video game for his mom and make everything okay. That Christmas Eve, his mom had the evening off to spend with him. They watched the movie 'A Christmas Story' on TV and when Ralphie got his BB gun, his mom turned off the TV and said, "I'm sorry that I don't get to see you very much and I know this isn't the newest and coolest, but I hope you like it." He opened up his Christmas gift and it was the original video gaming system, along with the original version of the game, that contained his favorite video game hero. The boy began to cry and gave his mom the deepest and longest hug he had ever given.

Matthew 22:36-39 (English Standard Version (ESV)- 2001- Crossway)
"Teacher, which is the great commandment in the Law?" And He said to him, "You shall love the Lord your God with all your heart and with all your soul and with all your mind. This is the great and first commandment. And a second is like it: You shall love your neighbor as yourself."

We all know people who are self-righteous and think that they are better than everyone. They go around thinking that they are the most important and that they know everything. It feels like you can't talk to them, because they don't listen or they don't even care. Those kinds of people are so frustrating. It gets under my skin the most when that person claims to be a Christian. They might hear you say a swear word, see you drink a beer, have a cigarette, and then see you as a lost soul, damned for hell. They aren't interested in hearing your story, or actually giving you the time of day. The self-righteous just see you as a lost soul needing to be saved. Christians, who preach that you need to be saved or you will be damned to the fires of hell, are not showing love. The core of the Christian faith is the greatest commandment.

Romans 2:1-3 (English Standard Version (ESV)- 2001- Crossway)
Therefore you have no excuse, O man, every one of you who judges. For in passing judgment on another you condemn yourself, because you, the judge, practice the very same things. We know the judgment of God rightly falls on those who practice such things. Do you suppose, O man- you who judge those who practice such things and yet do them yourself- that you will escape the judgment of God?

We all need to be saved. Not one of us, without Jesus, can stand before God the Father and receive salvation. We are saved through Jesus' death and resurrection. That is the price of grace. When Christians cast judgment, they are really casting judgment on themselves, because only God is the true Judge. Yes, I believe there is a hell, and yes, I believe God is just, but we can not pretend that we can be a perfect judge. There is no way that we could ever know the full picture of someone's life story. What they have been through or what they have felt. We could never be a just judge. Our duty is to love God with every part of who we are, and likewise love our fellow humans by showing them God's love for us. God is not interested in what good we think we are doing in the world, if we are doing it without a heart for others and without love.

1 Corinthians 13:1-3 (English Standard Version (ESV)- 2001- Crossway)
If I speak in the tongues of men and angels, but have not love, I am a noisy gong or a clanging cymbal. And if I have prophetic powers, and understand all mysteries and all knowledge, and if I have all faith, so as to remove mountains, but have not love, I am nothing. If I give away all I have, and if I deliver up my body to be burned, but have not love, I gain nothing.

So many people try to do good deeds, but for not the right

reasons. If you are doing good things to be recognised or rewarded, you are missing the point. If you are doing good in the world to earn something, you can never earn enough. Even if you try to share the Gospel, the love of Jesus, so that you can feel good about the difference that you are making, you have missed the point. We are to do good deeds out of selflessness, and most importantly, out of love for others. It is never about doing good in order to raise yourself up, or to earn something.

Philippians 1:15-18 (English Standard Version (ESV)- 2001- Crossway)
Some indeed preach Christ from envy and rivalry, but others from good will. The latter do it out of love, knowing that I am here for the defense of the Gospel. The former proclaim Christ out of rivalry, not sincerely but thinking to afflict me in my imprisonment.
What then? Only that in every way, whether in pretense or in truth, Christ is proclaimed, and in that I rejoice.

In chapter 5, I briefly talked about the religious division inside of the churches. So many churches claim to be spreading the Gospel and the love of Christ, while partaking in the divisions of church denominations, the theologies of the Arminian and the Calvonist doctrines (free will versus predestination doctrines), and baby baptisms versus adult baptisms. So many churches claim that they are serving God and spreading the good news of the Gospels. Instead of actually focusing on Jesus Christ, our Savior, they are casting judgment on others and are caught up in their own theologies. They are more concerned with giving the perfect sermons and singing the perfect songs, to get people inside of the church doors, instead of going out into the world and showing love. God isn't as concerned with theologies or church attendance, He is more concerned with the matters of our hearts. We should be reflecting on this question- 'Are we focused on ourselves or showing love?' I want to add that even though there are divisions within Christian churches, they are sharing the Gospel message, which is a good thing. My goal for addressing these divisions is that we, as Christians, should realize that they are not Christ-honoring.

Matthew 6:1-6 (English Standard Version (ESV)- 2001- Crossway)
Beware of practicing your righteousness before other people in order to be seen by them, for then you will have no reward from your Father who is in Heaven. Thus, when you give to the needy, sound no trumpet before you, as the hypocrites do in the synagogues and in the streets, that they may be praised by others. Truly, I say to you, they have received their reward. But when you give to the needy, do not let your left hand know what your right

hand is doing, so that your giving may be in secret. And your Father who sees in secret will reward you. And when you pray, you must not be like the hypocrites. For they love to stand and pray in the synagogues and at the street corners, that they may be seen by others. Truly, I say to you, they have received their reward. But when you pray, go into your room and shut the door and pray to your Father who is in secret. And your Father who sees in secret will reward you.

I think these verses in Matthew are so important and really reinforce my point. God isn't interested in you doing good things for the reason of being recognized, appreciated, or for making you feel like you have earned something. He is interested in your heart, your motives, and your love. You can be like an entrepreneur and give millions to the healthcare industry and even have hospitals change their names to yours. While giving away wealth to the healthcare industry is a noble thing, ultimately, seeking your name in lights and people's applause will be your only reward. God wants you to show love in a selfless way. He wants your love to be genuine and pure. Love that is focused on ourselves really isn't love at all.

Matthew 7:21-23 (English Standard Version (ESV)- 2001- Crossway)
Not everyone who says to me, 'Lord, Lord,' will enter the

kingdom of Heaven, but the one who does the will of My Father who is in Heaven. On that day many will say to Me, 'Lord, Lord, did we not prophesy in Your name, and cast out demons in Your name, and do many works in Your name?' And then will I declare to them, 'I never knew you; depart from Me, you workers of lawlessness.'

This set of verses used to give me nightmares. It scared me thinking that people who can prophesy, cast out demons, and do great things for God could still not be saved. It used to make me think that I sure as heck can't cast out demons, so what chance do I have to be saved? But as I got older and the further I got in my personal journey of faith, I realized that I don't actually have to cast out demons to know God. As we talked about with 1 Corinthians 13:1-3, we can do many great things, but without love, we gain nothing. We can go to church every Sunday, we can even be a pastor and study the word of God all day, every day, and still not have a relationship with Him. To have a relationship with God, we must accept that we are sinners and need to be saved by grace. We need to accept that Jesus died for our sins and that we must be born again. We then need to start the journey of faith and the sanctification process with a new heart. Our lives are not about us anymore. We can do good things without God, but we will never do great things. Great things happen when we are part of something bigger than ourselves, when we are a part of God's army, out loving people and saving souls. I don't know about you, but that's an army I want to be in and to fight for.

Ephesians 2:8-9 (English Standard Version (ESV)- 2001- Crossway)
For by grace you have been saved through faith. And this is not by your own doing; it is the gift of God, not a result of works, so that no one may boast.

As I wrap up this chapter, I want to regroup and say that there is no room for judgment in the Christian faith, because nothing that we could ever do could earn our salvation. There is no room to boast about how great we are or how much we have done. We are only saved by the death and resurrection of Jesus Christ, which was the price of saving grace. We are to believe and put our faith and hope in Jesus, to be born again. We are to love God and to love His creation. Are there times when we can call out people who are on the wrong path? Yes, of course, but we need to do it in love and in a caring, compassionate way. We are to correct others in a way that edifies the person and shows them love. We have all been that person needing correction, broken and in need of saving. We have the hope and the love of Jesus to be the light to guide our way.

CHAPTER NINE

DON'T DO THE JOURNEY ALONE

Ecclesiastes 4:9-10 (English Standard Version (ESV)- 2001- Crossway)
Two are better than one, because they have a good reward for their toil. For if they fall, one will lift up his fellow. But woe to him who is alone when he falls and has not another to lift him up!

The journey of faith and the sanctification process looks different for everyone. No individual is the same and every journey is unique. On that note, Just because you are on your own journey through this life, it doesn't mean that you have to do it alone, in fact, you are called for fellowship. We are called to be there to lift others up through their struggles and likewise, we are supposed to have others that we can rely on when we fall and need to be lifted up. We are not promised an easy journey in this life and there will be times when we will fall. The weight that we all carry is heavy. We can be strong and we will grow, but inevitably, there will be times that we need to lean on others.

Proverbs 27:17 (English Standard Version (ESV)- 2001- Crossway)
Iron sharpens iron, and one man sharpens another.

In this life, there will be plenty of people who come and go. For example, in high school you spend your four years with everyone in your grade, you go to classes with them, and build friendships with them. Everyone is trying to figure out who they are, their goals, passions, desires, and what they are going to do when they grow up. It is easy to think that, in the moment, those four years will never end, and these people that you are attending school with, will be there with you for your whole life. Then graduation comes, people start going to colleges, or they are starting their careers, and the next thing you know, the people that you grew up with aren't there for you. Sadly, it's just a part of life. That is why it is vitally important to make meaningful relationships where both people make an intentional effort, not only to keep the relationships going, but to build the relationships and make them grow. We are called to love our neighbor, all of the people that we come in contact with. Not everyone is supposed to be the person that you build a relationship with. When I say relationship, it can be the romantic relationship that leads to marriage, but also genuine friendships that become your accountability partners. Accountability partners are a type of relationship where you genuinely let that partner know how you are doing and they do the same. It's not just the generic, "Hey, how are you?", "I'm good, how are you?", "I'm good too, it was great catching up with you!" I'm talking about sharing how you are doing in your faith journey, any hardships that you may be having, how God is working in your life, the 'real' stuff. A person that you can trust to cry upon, tell that you're not doing okay, that you are struggling with things; such as depression, anxiety, hatred, grief, etc. This person should love you, honor you, respect you, not judge you, be there to encourage you, and help you grow. This person should trust you to be there for them as well. Like the verse in Proverbs says, we are called to sharpen one another.

In a romantic relationship, where you want to build a future that might lead to marriage, that person is your life partner, your priority. This is the relationship where you are to be the most open, honest, and intimate. In any romantic relationship there is the honeymoon phase, where you are infatuated with that person, every moment is a dream come true, and you want to spend all of your time with that person. I am by no means a relationship expert, but in every relationship, the honeymoon phase ends, complete infatuation fades, and the relationship deals with real life things. Not every moment is awesome, you have to deal with work, finances, housework, and all aspects of real life situations. This is an important, vital stage of the relationship. It takes hard work from both sides, but it leads to growth, and it is a beautiful thing. When going through tough times in the relationship, this is when you make damn sure that you make the extra effort to keep your partner your priority. During the difficult times, give your partner special and romantic surprises. Make time to still go on dates and have fun together. Be sure to remind them how much that you love and treasure them and let them know that you are proud of them. Little random words of love and encouragement mean more than you know. In romantic relationships, there will be difficult times, you will get on each other's nerves, and times that you will let each other down. We have to remember that as humans, we will never be perfect and we will never measure up. We will grow and make progress, but we will never be perfect. That is why it is essential to make God your first love and to show grace. As God loves sinners like us and saves us freely, we are called to show that to others, especially to your romantic partner. Your romantic partner is your lover, your soulmate, and your best friend. That is why it's the most important relationship for growth with each other, extending much grace and mercy towards one another.

In your other relationships and friendships, you need to make an effort to support and encourage them in their faith, in their journeys, and they should do likewise. As I said previously, friends will let you down at times and you will disappoint them as well, because we are imperfect humans in need of grace. We need to build each other up and encourage one another. These deep-rooted relationships are where we can lovingly discuss the aspects of our lives that could use improvement. It is so important to do this out of love and not judgment. It is strictly out of a place of encouragement and support that produces growth in the relationship. In all relationships, the most important thing is to show God's love towards them

Galatians 6:2 (English Standard Version (ESV)- 2001- Crossway)
Bear one another's burdens, and so fulfill the law of Christ.

If someone you know is really struggling, we are called to be there for them. There are real pains and struggles in this world. People who have lost loved ones, people who have been hurt emotionally, physically, sexually, mentally, abused, abandoned, homeless, sick, diseased, etc. We live in a broken world and there are times when the struggles seem too much to bear. Every person deals with their own internal battles of low self-worth, depression, anxiety, brokenness, abandonment, loneliness, hatred, guilt, and pain. It is easy to feel unworthy and unloved. So many times, people believe that no one cares and that they have to deal with things all alone. This is a reason that we are called not to judge. We will never know what people are going through internally. We need to be there for people and to show them God's love. We need to remind people that they are not a mistake.

Psalm 139:13-14 (English Standard Version (ESV)- 2001- Crossway)
For you formed my inward parts; you knitted me together in my mother's womb. I praise you, for I am fearfully and wonderfully made. Wonderful are your works; my soul knows it very well.

We are not a mistake. God created us with a plan and a purpose in mind. We need to know that it is alright to feel pain, it is good to cry, so that we are able to heal. We need to know that we are not alone. God wants a relationship with each and every one of us and no one is too far from His embrace. Jesus took our burdens, our pain, and our suffering on the Cross, so that we can be set free. We don't have to carry the burdens alone. We need to break the stigma of it being a weakness to show emotions. Suicide rates are escalating, especially through the COVID-19 pandemic, because people feel alone. People feel like they are a burden and that others are better off without them. Men, especially, feel like they need to "man up" when it comes to their mental health. Something needs to change. Going to counseling and therapy isn't a shameful thing to do. There are professionals that understand what we are going through and can honestly help. We, as people, can spare a little time to check on our friends. We should see how they are really doing, not a superficial, "Hey, what's up?" Be more intentional, making sure that they know that you truly want to listen to them, that you care about how they are doing, and that you are not there to judge them. If people did more intentional reaching out, I believe that would make a powerful difference. I also want to address that as you should do that for others, it is just as important that you have that person who will do this for you. In a one-sided relationship, it can be draining for that person who always seems to be the one who gives the shirt off their back. Sometimes you need that shirt, sometimes you need that support. It is important to have a two-way street. The greatest commandment states to love your neighbor as yourself, that means you have to experience love yourself, so that you can love others.

Hebrews 10:24-25 (English Standard Version (ESV)- 2001- Crossway)
And let us consider how to stir up one another to love and good works, not neglecting to meet together, as it is the habit of some, but encouraging one another, and all the more as you see the Day drawing near.

The importance of having relationships start with building up and encouraging each other in life and in faith, but then there is a next step. We need to push each other into doing good works in the world. The most important thing is to inspire each other to love others more deeply and to share the good news of Jesus Christ. Jesus didn't live a safe life. He stirred up the religious and government systems. He taught us how to live and what God expects from us. He lived as a servant and He then died, so that we may live. We are not meant to live safe lives that are focused on ourselves. Jesus promised that He would come again and that we must be ready. It is so important to have Godly fellowship, in order to encourage and grow with each other. It is easy to get caught up in the day-to-day activities, where we lose focus on the bigger picture. Whether it be a church setting, Bible studies, or just hanging-out, we are called to not neglect fellowship, so that we can be encouraged to stay on the right path and focus on doing God's work. We should be focused on studying God's word, be growing in our love for God, and for our neighbors. In this life, we will never love God perfectly, and we will never love others perfectly. That is why we need to continue on the faith journey and the sanctification process. We live in a broken, sinful world, and we will never be without sin. If we focus on God, continue to be in His word, remain in Christian fellowship, then we will grow, and we will make progress.

Matthew 18:20 (English Standard Version (ESV)- 2001- Crossway)
For where two or three are gathered in My name, there am I among them.

Jesus promises us that when we gather in fellowship, He is there with us in Spirit. He sees and hears us. He understands what we are going through and sees our growth. He knows our hearts and hears our prayers.

Jeremiah 29:11 (English Standard Version (ESV) 2001- Crossway)
For I know the plans I have for you, declares the Lord, plans for welfare and not for evil, to give you a future and a hope.

As it reads in my Bible commentary (English Standard Version (ESV)- 2001- Crossway), 'Welfare' in Hebrew is the word 'Shalom' and the commentary says, "Which covers all aspects of peace and plenty." God is not some form of the ancient god, Zeus, waiting to strike us with lightning bolts when we disappoint or anger Him. He loves us and cares for us. He wants our peace and cares about our future. He wants to offer us hope. God wants a relationship with us, so much so, that He sent His Son in our place, so that we have a way to spend eternity with Him. God is invested in us through His creation and through mankind. He loves us deeply, promising to be there for us, and through our fellowship. He celebrates our progress and our growth. He hears our prayers and will always answer them, in His way and in His timing. We should be excited about sharing that with others. We should be excited to dig into fellowship in order to grow in our faith. We have access to God's words through the scriptures of the Bible, and we should be excited to dig in and study them. I want to note that it does take studying. The Bible was written by men, who were guided by the Holy Spirit. It was written for us, but not directly to us, as it was written in the author's time in history, for the times and circumstances that they were in. We need to interpret what was written within context and then determine how it applies to us. That is why it is important to study and discuss the scriptures with others, as Jesus promises to be there in our fellowship. We can ask Him to help make the scriptures clear to us, how we can grow deeper in our love for God, deeper in the understanding of His words, and deeper in our love for others.

John 15:12-17 (English Standard Version (ESV)- 2001- Crossway)
"This is My commandment, that you love one another as I have loved you. Greater love has no one than this, that someone lays down his life for his friends. You are My friends if you do what I command you. No longer do I call you servants, for the servant does not know what his master is doing, but I have called you friends, for all that I have heard from my Father I have made known to you. You did not choose Me but I chose you and appointed you that you should go and bear fruit and that your fruit should abide, so that whatever you ask the Father in My name, He may give it to you. These things I command you, so that you will love one another."

One of my all time favorite bands called, 'The Color Morale', released a music video that always makes me emotional enough to cry. The music video is for the song titled, 'Strange Comfort.' The music video has a story line of two soldiers. One soldier had a bullet wound from battle and the other soldier is carrying him on his shoulders through deep, snowy terrain, trying to get to safety. There is a point in the video where the soldier leans the injured soldier against a tree to rest. The injured soldier was crying and took out his pistol, pointed it to his own chest, and signaled to the other soldier to relieve him of his pain. The soldier couldn't bring himself to do it, so he put his head up to the injured soldier's head. He aimed the pistol against his head to project the bullet through both of their heads. He did this out of desperation, because he couldn't bear the thought of going on without his friend, the injured soldier. Both soldiers were crying and he finally pulled the pistol away from his head, lifted the injured soldier off of the ground, and continued to carry him. That video was remarkable, showing true brotherly love.

Have you ever loved someone so much that you couldn't bear the thought of not having them in your life? Have you ever loved someone so deeply that you would give up your life for them? Jesus, the Son of God, loved us so much that He came down to this broken and sinful world to die for us, because He couldn't bear the thought of not spending eternity with us. He was willing to bear our sins and He took our place on that Cross, withstanding the strikes of a thorned whip, nails going through His hands and feet, and death on the Cross, so that we would have eternal life. The price of our Salvation is more than we could ever pay and we were given it freely. The depths of God's love for us is more than we could ever understand. Jesus says in John 15:12-17 that there is no greater love than laying your life down for your friends. That is what Jesus has done for us, and that is what we are called to do for others. We don't have to literally die for someone, but we are called to have that kind of love and put loving others ahead of ourselves. As we have been loved and saved by God's grace, we are to show that love to others. We are to let others know that there is love, hope, and a future beyond the darkness and brokenness of this world. When the Bible talks about the importance of fellowship, we are to take that seriously. Our relationships are to be so strong that we should be willing to lay our lives down for them. We are to be rooted with love, ingrained in the fiber of our beings. As Christians, we are to be born again, and put to death our sinful desires. We should have the desire to grow in our relationship with God and to pursue righteousness. We shouldn't try to force Jesus down people's throats, but show them how beautiful the journey is walking with Him. We have a hope and a future that goes beyond this broken world. Jesus laid His life down for us, so that we can show that same love towards others.

CHAPTER TEN

LET THE PAST BE THE PAST, COME HOME

Luke 15:11-32 (English Standard Version (ESV)- 2001- Crossway)

And He said, "There was a man who had two sons. And the younger of them said to his father, 'Father, give me the share of property that is coming to me.' And he divided his property between them. Not many days later, the younger son gathered all he had and took a journey into a far country, and there he squandered his property in reckless living. And when he had spent everything, a severe famine arose in that country, and he began to be in need. So he went and hired himself out to one of the citizens of that country, who sent him into his fields to feed pigs. And he was longing to be fed with the pods that the pigs ate, and no one gave him anything. But when he came to himself, he said 'How many of the father's hired servants have more than enough bread, but I perish here with hunger! I will arise and go to my father, and I will say to him, "Father, I have sinned against Heaven and before you. I am no longer worthy to be called your son. Treat me as one of your hired servants." And he arose and came to his father. But while he was still a long way off, his father saw him and felt compassion, and ran and embraced him and kissed him. And the son said to him, 'Father, I have sinned against Heaven and before you. I am no longer worthy to be called your son.' But the father said to his servants, 'Bring quickly the best robe, and put it on him, and put a ring on his hand, and shoes on his feet. And bring the fattened calf and kill it, and let us eat and celebrate. For this my son was dead and is alive again; he was lost, and is found.' And they began to celebrate. Now his older son was in the field, and as he came and drew near to the house, he heard music and dancing. And he called one of the servants and asked what these things meant. And he said to him, 'Your brother has come, and your father has killed the fattened calf, because he has received him back safe and sound.' But he was angry and refused to go in. His father came out and entreated him, but he answered his father, 'Look, these many years I have served you, and I never disobeyed your command, yet you never gave me a young goat, that I might celebrate with my friends. But when this son of yours came, who has devoured your property with prostitutes, you killed the fattened calf for him?' And he said to him, 'Son, you are always with me, and all that is mine is yours. It was fitting to celebrate and be glad, for this your brother was dead, and is alive; he was lost, and is found.'"

This is a powerful story of love and redemption. A story of someone seeking the pleasures of life, only caring for themselves, and then realizing that way of living leads to a dead end. All of the riches and pleasures that he could have asked for, eventually lead him to a path that made him lower than human. Can you imagine getting so desperate for food that you would consider eating with pigs? This son so desperately wanted to pursue his own pleasures and desires, that he asked for his share of his father's inheritance. I can only imagine the pain and the heartbreak that his father had. The father loved his sons and gave them everything they needed. I'm sure the sons did have to do hard work, but they wanted for nothing. I can also imagine the older brother's frustration, because he always stayed in line, did his work, and honored his father. He felt like he couldn't even celebrate with his friends, because of his hard work and responsibilities. I'm sure that his work load didn't lighten when his younger brother left and partied away the inheritance. The difficult thing to imagine is how the father reacted when seeing his son come home. Despite the anger, the pain, and the heartbreak, the father saw his son and embraced him. The younger son knew how wrong he was and understood that he was not worthy of forgiveness, but what he received was way more than he ever expected. He received unconditional love and was welcomed with celebration. Not only was he welcomed home, he was given jewelry, the finest clothes, and the grandest feast. The father wasn't ignorant to what his son had been doing, and he was hurt, but when he saw his son in his brokenness with a change of heart, he didn't dwell on his son's mistakes, he didn't scold him, he let the past be the past, and welcomed him home. His father knew that he had been lost and now he was found. His soul was dead and now it was alive. The son didn't deserve the love and celebration, and the son knew that, but it was given to him anyway. He truly received grace. His heart had been redeemed.

I know in my past, I have been that younger son. I was raised by parents who loved me, cared for me, and wanted the best for me. I was raised to know the difference between right and wrong. I was taught the importance of loving God and following His commandments. Even though today, I know that I don't agree with everything that my parents believe, I at least know that I was raised by parents who love me. I had the love of God anchored in my heart and I am forever grateful. Growing up, I really did have a rebellious stage. I sought after my own pleasures and got heavy into partying. I was to the point where I was getting very drunk every single night and I became addicted to porn, which led me down some dark paths. There are a lot of things I regret. The path that I was on really affected my self-worth and self-esteem. I was supposed to have been a great man of God who impacted people for Jesus, telling others how I overcame my speech impediment, and led many to Christ. Instead, I was a disaster, a broken mess. I thank God every day that He put the right people and friends into my life and of course for my amazing girlfriend, Debby. All of the people that God placed in my life, helped give me a wake-up call, reminding me of my worth, and that God wanted more for me than the path that I was on. God never left me and welcomed me back with an unconditional embrace. If I would have stayed on that path, I don't know if I would be here today. Instead, God rained blessings down into my life, and every day gives me more than I deserve. I have the woman of my dreams. Debby and I share the love of music, movies, watching football, playing pool, celebrating holidays, appreciate spending quality time together, and most importantly our love for God. We both have overcome our pasts by the grace of God and have found true, deep-rooted love in each other. He blessed me with friends that deeply love me, believe in me, and support me. God blessed me with the gift of writing, a deep love, and a heart for people. I'm so grateful for all of the blessings I have had in my life and continue to receive. It's crazy that my girlfriend and I are home owners, business owners, and are about to have a beautiful commitment ceremony, that is dedicating our relationship to God. It's crazy that I am writing my fifth published book. With every book that I write, I am learning and growing in my faith. I remember going through speech therapy, and I remember my parents reading books to me for school, because it was a struggle for me to read. Since then, I have accomplished being a vocalist of a band, a spoken word poet, a podcaster, and a published author. God uses imperfect, broken people to share His message and His love with this broken and imperfect world. Have you reached a point where you feel that you are too far gone? Do you feel lost or broken? Do you feel unworthy, or too messed up for

God, or even people to love you? I promise you that you are not too far gone. I promise you that God has never left you. He is waiting for you with arms wide open, longing to embrace you, and welcome you home. He wants your heart and for you to give faith a chance. He understands the pain, the struggles, and He still unconditionally loves you. He is ready to put the past behind and to celebrate you. He wants to bless you more than you could ever imagine and to throw the craziest party Heaven has ever seen! God is your Heavenly Father, He created you, knows you, and actually loves you. He doesn't make empty promises and He is there for you. God is on your side and is cheering you on. Nothing you can do will ever make Him love you any less.

Romans 8:37-39 (English Standard Version (ESV)- 2001- Crossway)
No, in all these things we are more than conquerors through Him who loved us. For I am sure that neither death nor life, nor angels nor rulers, nor things present nor things to come, nor powers, nor height nor depth, nor anything else in all creation, will be able to separate us from the love of God in Christ Jesus our Lord.

Nothing, and I mean nothing, can prevent God from loving you. That includes you! Nothing you can do can stop God from loving you. No matter how far you run,

God will never leave your side. No matter how deep you are into addiction, no matter who has walked away, no matter how broken you are, God is still there for you with His arms wide open, ready to embrace you, and walk with you through the healing process. No matter what life throws at you, whether that be hate, prejudice, judgment, guilt, poverty, homelessness, sickness, shame, abuse; nothing can separate us from the love of God. Through our walk with God, we can heal, overcome, and conquer anything that comes against us. Jesus will walk on water, feed hundreds of people from a couple of fish and loaves of bread, make the blind see, heal leprosy, turn over tables at religious gatherings, sit with sinners, raise people from the dead. He will do the impossible to show us that His saving grace is, in fact, possible and His unconditional love is indeed true.

I want you to imagine a woman in her 20's, she has never felt loved in her entire life. She was raised by an alcoholic father, who beat on her mom every night when he got drunk. The only way her mom knew how to cope was with pills. One night, when the girl was 17, the drinking got so bad that her mom committed suicide by using those pills. The girl was so distraught that she ran away. She started seeing a guy that she had met while living in a hotel room, and eventually she got pregnant. When the guy found out that she was pregnant, he just left her. She knew she couldn't afford to be a single mom, she was struggling to survive as it was, on her own. She felt like there was no other option, but to get an abortion. After she went through with the abortion, she felt so much guilt and shame. She started drinking heavily to numb her pain. One night, she drank so much that the police were called and she was transported by an ambulance to the hospital, to get her stomach pumped. After she had recovered, she knew she needed help. She knew that she couldn't keep going on like this. Her hotel was near a church and she decided that she was going to give it a try. On the next Sunday morning, she snuck into the church and found a seat in the back row. She had never heard music like what she was hearing. The songs were so uplifting and spoke of the unconditional love from the Heavenly Father. She never knew unconditional love, or never had any sense of real love, and definitely not from a father figure. When the music stopped, the pastor came up to give a sermon about a shepherd. The shepherd had left his flock of 99 sheep to find a single, lost sheep. Then the pastor compared the shepherd to Jesus, searching for that one lost soul. He then talked about how, in his past, he was lost in a lifestyle of sex, drugs, and rock and roll. He was in a touring band and he fell deep into drugs and alcohol, to the point where he overdosed and could have died. During his recovery, he found Jesus and turned his life around. She knew she wanted to experience that kind of life change. As the last song played, she broke down and cried so hard, the tears wouldn't stop. As she was bawling, a man came asking if he could pray for her. After his prayer, he invited her to go to a young adult Bible Study. She hesitantly said yes and was willing to give it a try. After a few times, she started feeling really connected. She eventually asked Jesus to be her Savior. At the next group meeting, she decided to tell the group her life's story, about her alcoholic dad, her mom's addiction to pills, and her mom's death by overdose. After running away, she got pregnant, had her abortion, and then drank to the point of needing her stomach pumped. After sharing her story, she felt really relieved, yet really vulnerable. Then something horrible happened. A member of the group judged her harshly and told her that she was going to hell for having an abortion. She broke down and ran out of the church. All of the pain of her past came flooding back, she wanted to feel numb again, to stop feeling. She had put her trust in the people of this church and had felt like she had found a place where she could belong, but then this happened. She ran to a liquor store and bought a bottle of booze. She found herself drinking on a bridge, looking down at the traffic that was below her. She felt hopeless, unloved, and unworthy. She cursed at God, blaming Him for everything that happened. She didn't want to be in this cruel world, with a God that hated her. She started climbing over the ledge of the bridge, getting ready to jump. She noticed the man that she had first met at the church, who had invited her to the Bible Study. He screamed at her, begging her to get off the bridge. He climbed up after her and took her hand to get her off of the ledge. He sincerely apologized for the words that were said to her were so wrong. He told her that God loves her unconditionally and has a plan for her life. He then asked her to let him prove it to her and she hesitantly agreed. They got into his car, and the next thing she knows, they are at the house where she grew up and where her dad is still living. He told her to please sit and wait, because she did not want to go in. He knocks on the door and she sees her father in the doorway. She decides to step out of the car, her dad runs to her, drops to his knees, and weeps. Through his tears, her father says, "I am so sorry for everything. I was a broken man when your mother and you left, I lost everything. I know I don't deserve this, but will you please, please forgive me?" They were both weeping, she embraced him, they hugged and they hugged, and they cried until there were no more tears, and then cried some more. It turns out, that her dad had attempted suicide when she left and then he was arrested, went through treatment, and found God. He started attending the church that she had found, as well. Of course, they both had work to do, but with God's love and grace, they found their way back to each other.

God sees the struggles and the pain that you are going through. He understands the brokenness. Jesus knows your innermost being and weeps when you weep. He is waiting for you with arms opened wide, longing for your embrace. God knows when we are lost and spiritually dead, and He rejoices when you come back to Him. He wants to let the past be the past and welcome you home. When the world turns its back on you, Jesus is there with arms wide open. His love for you is unconditional. You are loved!

CHAPTER ELEVEN

FIGHT THE GOOD FIGHT AND FINISH STRONG

1 Corinthians 13:4-8,13 (English Standard Version (ESV)- 2001- Crossway)
"Love is patient and kind; love does not envy or boast; it is not arrogant or rude. It does not insist on its own way; it is not irritable or resentful; it does not rejoice at wrongdoing, but rejoices with the truth. Love bears all things, believes all things, hopes all things, endures all things. Love never ends. As for prophecies, they will pass away; as for tongues, they will cease; as for knowledge, it will pass away." "So now faith, hope, and love abide, these three; but the greatest of these is love."

These verses are common Bible verses that are used in weddings. Of course, these verses are great verses for married couples to live by, but they are also meant for Christians to live by, on their faith journey. Love is the core of the Christian faith. Love should be in the fiber of our beings. With the exception of the last verse, I want you to re-read these verses replacing the word 'love' with 'A Christian.' I will re-write these verses down below so that we can go through it together.

1 Corinthians 13:4-8 (revised version of verses from- English Standard Version (ESV)- 2001- Crossway)

"**A Christian** is patient and kind; **A Christian** does not envy or boast; **A Christian** is not arrogant or rude. **A Christian** does not insist on **A Christian's** own way; **A Christian** is not irritable or resentful; **A Christian** does not rejoice at wrongdoing, but rejoices with the truth. **A Christian** bears all things, believes all things, hopes all things, endures all things. **A Christian** never ends. As for prophecies, they will pass away; as for tongues, they will cease; as for knowledge, it will pass away."

As we journey through this life, making our way through the sanctification process, we need to strive to make love the core of who we are. We need to constantly ask ourselves if we are measuring up to God's commands. Are we being patient and kind? Do we envy or boast? Are we being arrogant or rude? Do we insist on our own way? Are we being irritable or resentful? Are we rejoicing in wrongdoing or are we rejoicing in truth? Are we bearing, believing, hoping, and enduring all things? We have to remember that our souls will never end, even when the things of this world pass away. We should not be wrapped up in prophecies, our bodies, or our knowledge, because they are not eternal. Our souls are eternal, we need to make sure that our souls are on the right path, following our Creator. We are called to have faith, hope, and love, because these will abide, or stay. Out of faith, hope, and love, love is the greatest. As I have repeatedly discussed in this book, we will never be perfect. There will be times when we will not be patient or kind. There will be times when we will insist on our own way, and there will be times when we don't rejoice in the truth. As we grow in our relationship with God, we continue on the sanctification process, and we will slowly become a better example of love. We will be more patient and kind. We will be less arrogant and we won't need to insist on our own way. As there are plenty of bumps in the road, there are plenty of successful moments. There will be times when you take steps back, but God is right there with you and every step is progress. There will be times when people will say that you are making mistakes, you will face judgment, but remember every faith journey is different. The only relationship that truly matters is your personal relationship with God. Remember, you don't have to be perfect to make a difference. We follow the One who is perfect and we are called to reflect His love. As long as we are growing in our faith, and staying on the journey, God will use us in His master plan. God doesn't use perfect people. He tends to use the meek, the humble, the broken, and the imperfect, to show His greatness, His compassion, and His love.

John 14:12-14 (English Standard Version (ESV)- 2001- Crossway)
"Truly, truly, I say to you, whoever believes in Me will also do the works that I do; and greater works than these will he do, because I am going to the Father. Whatever you ask in My name, this I will do, that the Father may be glorified in the Son. If you ask Me anything in My name, I will do it."

Jesus knew that His time was limited on this Earth. He wouldn't be able to be there in person with everyone who was to be upon this Earth. That is why we are to continue on with His work, as we have been handed the torch. Even though Jesus isn't physically here, He never truly left. He is here and He is with us by His spirit. He hears our prayers and promises to meet our needs. When He said that we could ask Him for anything, that doesn't mean we can ask Him for a get rich quick plan or anything else, due to selfishness, because that is not the point. We can expect that He will give us what we need to advance His kingdom and glorify the Father. Are Christians ever blessed financially? There are Christians that have been blessed financially. Financial blessings are not always a bad thing. The difference is that they are called to bless others with that gift. I am gifted with my writing and it would be wrong to not use my gift to bless others. We all have different blessings or gifts and we are all called to use them to love others. If we use our gifts selfishly, no matter what the gift is, we are not serving God and loving others. When we genuinely ask God to build us up in our faith, to have the strength, the materials, or even the people to gather around us to help advance the good news of the Gospel, God does hear us and promises to meet our needs.

Romans 10:14-15 (English Standard Version (ESV)- 2001- Crossway)
How then will they call on Him in whom they have not believed? And how are they to believe in Him of whom

they have never heard? And how are they to hear without someone preaching? And how are they to preach unless they are sent? As it is written, "How beautiful are the feet of those who preach the good news!"

In my life and my experiences, especially with all the different kinds of people I have encountered, I have never been an advocate for shoving the Bible down people's throats. In America, unless you have somehow managed to live in a bunker and avoid the government, you have probably heard of God and Christianity. Since I have moved to a really small South Dakota town, I mean such a small town that people who live in the big cities along the coasts such as San Francisco, California and New York City, probably could not imagine, in their wildest dreams, that a town this small could ever exist. I have learned that every town, no matter how small, contains a church, a post office, and a bar. There is actually one town that I have been to that doesn't even have a post office, but they do have a church and a bar. My point being, I don't believe that you could live in America and not have a knowledge of God or Christianity. I believe the biggest problem is that 'Christians' represent Jesus in such a way that it leaves them having a bad taste in their mouth. Concerning these verses in Romans, I believe it is vitally important that we show love and respect towards others. We have to build relationships with people and show Jesus to them in a new light, in a way that they haven't heard about Jesus before. In showing people how God has changed your life and saved you, people can see the beauty of God and His love for them, in a way that they have never seen before. When they see how amazing God is, we pray that God softens their heart towards Him and creates real change. I believe it is our goal to fulfill the verses in Romans 10:14-15, not in a religious or judgmental way, but to actually show them the love of Jesus and that starts with a relationship. People don't get saved by attending church or by threatening hell if they don't believe. People get saved when they believe that Jesus loved them so much that He died on their behalf. We have the free gift of saving grace. We are sinners in need of saving and God sent His Son on our behalf, so that we don't have to go to hell and we can spend eternity with Him in Heaven. We need to spread the good news of the Gospel, by extending God's grace and love towards them. As I stated in my previous book, 'Imperfectly Spreading A Perfect Gospel', in chapter two, "Love speaks way deeper than condemnation ever will." When we spread the love of Christ, that is truly when the good news of the Gospel is being shared, and that is when, as it says in Romans, "How beautiful are the feet of those who preach the good news!"

John 14:25-27 (English Standard Version (ESV)- 2001- Crossway)

"These things I have spoken to you while I am still with you. But the Helper, the Holy Spirit, whom the Father will send in My name, He will teach you all things and bring to your remembrance all that I have said to you. Peace I leave with you; My peace I give to you. Not as the world gives do I give you. Let not your hearts be troubled, neither let them be afraid."

When Jesus was preparing to depart from the world and His disciples, He was teaching and instructing about the Holy Spirit. In the Christian faith, God is made of three parts, otherwise known as the God-Head. The God-Head includes God the Father, God the Son, and God the Holy Spirit. Believe me when I say that I am not the most intelligent person to try to explain to you all the theology that goes into the God-Head. I'm sure there are plenty of scholarly books and lectures on the God-Head and I'm not going to try to act like I have got it all figured out. All I know is that there is a God-Head and it includes God the Father, God the Son, and God the Holy Spirit. They are all equally God, all are perfect and Holy, and they are all involved in our Salvation. Before Jesus departed, He promised His disciples and all of us that the Holy Spirit would come into our lives, guide us, teach us, and remind us all of Jesus' teachings. As Jesus promises us in *John 14:18*

(English Standard Version (ESV)- 2001- Crossway), "I will not leave you as orphans." He promises the Holy Spirit would come to us. When it comes to our faith journey and the sanctification process, we do not have to face it alone. We have the Holy Spirit in us, teaching us, and guiding us. Just as in the beginning, God didn't force Adam and Eve into obeying Him, but gave them free will. The Holy Spirit doesn't force us to do anything, but instead, is there to help us to grow in our faith and to guide us along the faith journey. With the help of the Holy Spirit, we can fight our sin nature, fight the good fight of faith, grow in holiness, deepen our love of God, and strengthen our love for others. The Holy Spirit loves us deeply and unconditionally. The Holy Spirit is a part of God, whose love is perfect and unconditional. The Holy Spirit celebrates our growth and makes clear the path of our faith journey. When we are born again, the Holy Spirit is with us always. The Holy Spirit will never leave us and we can always trust in Him.

Matthew 28:18-20 (English Standard Version (ESV)- 2001- Crossway)
And Jesus came and said to them, "All authority in Heaven and on Earth has been given to Me. Go therefore and make disciples of all nations, baptizing them in the name of the Father and of the Son and of the Holy Spirit, teaching them to observe all that I have commanded you.

And behold, I am with you always, to the end of the age."

When Jesus left this world to ascend to Heaven, after His death and resurrection, I'm sure it was scary, confusing, and intimidating, for the disciples. Jesus came and turned the world upside down. He taught in opposition to what the Pharisees and Saducess (the religious leaders) were teaching, He befriended sinners, healed the sick, gave sight to the blind, walked on water, raised the dead to life, and so much more. He then commanded His disciples to continue His legacy, handing them His torch. He gave the disciples the duty of the Great Commission, spreading the good news of the Gospel into all of the world. That is a daunting task, but then He promises that He is with us always, to the end of the age. Of course, Jesus' disciples aren't alive today and our mission is to carry the torch as well. Making disciples is not an overnight process. Jesus spent His entire ministry with the same twelve guys. Literally, for His entire ministry they were homeless, traveling on foot, from town to town, teaching, healing, and blessing others. Jesus fed into the lives of the disciples for years. We are commanded to make disciples, which means pouring into the lives of others, teaching them the ways of Jesus, loving them, and blessing them. When we make disciples, it is our hope that they will go and do likewise. As I said earlier, we don't need to shove Jesus down people's throats. That is why it is so important to build relationships. That is how we spread the good news of the Gospel. We need to devote our lives to loving God and loving others. We need to build relationships and offer grace. We need to meet people where they are at and listen to them. We need to let people know that they are not alone and that there is a God, who sent His only Son, who took our sins and died on a Cross so that we can live. When we accept Jesus as our Savior, we are born again and we are given new desires. This life isn't about us anymore. Our lives are devoted to God and to our neighbor- our fellow beings. Our biggest treasure isn't winning first place, but being there with our fellow teammates making sure that we all get to the finish line.

It is definitely bittersweet wrapping up this book. I have spent hours every week in a coffee shop, digging into the Bible and learning, myself, how to grow in my faith, my love for God, my love for others, and hopefully, encouraging my fellow readers on their faith journey. The writing process really strengthens my faith and allows me to use my gifts to encourage others. I love hearing stories of how my gift has helped, encouraged, and inspired others. I hope you will be encouraged to use your gifts for God and for others. I want to make sure that I say to my readers who are not of the Christian faith, thank you for sticking with me through this journey. If what I have written and shared is not your truth, that is totally alright. There is no judgment here. I just want you to know that you are loved and accepted in this community. Maybe, something that I have said makes you look at Jesus and the Christian faith in a different light, or a different way. Maybe, something you have read changes your perspective from what you grew up hearing about God, that made you feel judged or condemned. Many times, God is portrayed as a Zeus figure, just waiting for you to take a wrong step and then will strike you down with a lightning bolt. That is not the god I follow. At the end of the day, I just want you to know that you are loved and accepted. If you have any questions or concerns, please feel free to reach out. Thank you for making it through this book. I love you all.

As I wrap up, I want to thank you all for picking up this book and for all of your love and support. It was a crazy journey accomplishing writing this book in about three months. It has been a weird time in my life, not being employed under an employer, and starting up a cleaning business. It has tested my faith in trusting God to provide for me, but also gave me the opportunity to have a lot of time to pump out this book. If I could do this for a living, I definitely would not hate that idea. I also want to thank my amazing girlfriend, Debby, for believing in me, trusting in me to not be employed, starting up the cleaning business, and for the time I have been given to write this book. I hope you, the reader, are challenged, encouraged, and most of all, know that you are loved. Remember, there is nothing that we can do to earn our salvation, we are saved by God's unconditional love. Sending His one and only Son to die for our sins, so that we can have eternal life with Him in Paradise. Our mission in this life is to love God and others. I also want to encourage you in your faith journey, to grow and finish strong. We will never be perfect. We may take one step forward and two steps back, but every step is progress. We will never love God perfectly, we will never love others perfectly, but as we continue on the faith journey, we will become sanctified by the grace of God. Remember, to never take this journey alone. Grow in fellowship and love with each other. Get into studying the word of God, becoming more sanctified in truth, and love. Grow in your love for God and others, daily. Use your gifts and passions to love God and love your neighbor. God uses broken and imperfect people, of which I am one, to share the good news of the Gospel.

I want to encourage you by sharing what I have been through, one more time. I have lived far from a perfect life. I had to overcome a speech impediment, which made it a struggle for me to speak or even to read. I have overcome addictions to alcohol and pornography. I was a broken man and God chose to use me. God used my imperfections and now I am a published author, a spoken word poet, and a podcaster. I am not perfect. I am still just a tattooed, metalhead, white guy that loves Jesus. God saw through my mess, loves me, blesses me, and uses me to spread His perfect love in this world. If God could save and use a broken and imperfect person like me, I promise that He can use a person like you. God loves you and has a plan and a purpose for your life. Just put your faith in Him and experience the wild ride. Through the love of Jesus, we are a beacon of hope and the light in the darkness.

Amen.

SAVING GRACE

IT'S NOT ABOUT YOU ANYMORE

CREDITS

English Standard Version (ESV)- 2001- Crossway - Every
Bible Verse Used Throughout

CHAPTER ONE
John 3:16-21

Movie - A Christmas Story

Oxford Languages on Google Dictionary -
Christian definition of 'grace'
Romans 3:10-12

CHAPTER TWO
Luke 5:1-11

John 7:53-8:11

Luke 19:1-10

CHAPTER THREE
Matthew 25:35-46

James 1:19-20

John 3:12-17

Former President Trump

Movie - Peanut Butter Falcon

Matthew 5:43-44

Matthew 20:1-16

Charles Dickens - A Christmas Carol

Matthew 6:25-34

CHAPTER SEVEN

Matthew 18:1-4

Philippians 2:3-8

Romans 12:16

Oxford Languages on Google Dictionary -
Definition of 'haughty'

CHAPTER EIGHT

Matthew 7:1-5

The Happy Givers Ministry - created by Carlos A.
Rodriques

Matthew 25:35-46

Movie - A Christmas Story

Romans 2:1-3

Matthew 22:36-39

1 Corinthians 13:1-3

Philippians 1:15-18

Matthew 6:1-6

Matthew 7:21-23

Ephesians 2:8-9

Happy Givers Ministry - two sweatshirt quotes -
"If you hate anyone because of your faith, you're doing it wrong.", "Jesus is the refugee, the man on death row, the child at the border, the single mom with two jobs, the person with a disability, the friend with an addiction, the transgender co-worker, the kid with no lunch money. How you treat them is how you treat Jesus."

Band - August Burns Red's lyrics from the song 'Provision'- "I'm just as much the problem as the man behind bars. He did with his business what I do in my heart."

CHAPTER NINE

Ecclesiastes 4:9-10

Proverbs 27:17

Galatians 6:2

Psalm 139:13-14

Hebrews 10:24-25

Matthew 18:20

Jeremiah 29:11- with Bible commentary of definition of "welfare" (English Standard Version (ESV)- 2001- Crossway)

John 15:12-17

Band - The Color Morale -

Music video reference from song 'Strange Comfort'

CHAPTER TEN
Luke 15:11-32

Romans 8:37-39

CHAPTER ELEVEN
1 Corinthians 13:4-8,13

John 14:12-14

Romans 10:14-15

Book- Quote from 'Imperfectly Spreading A Perfect Gospel' -

"Love speaks way deeper than condemnation ever will."

John 14:25-27

John 14:18

Matthew 28:18-20

ABOUT THE AUTHOR BACK COVER PHOTO
"unworthy." sweatshirt - from the band Convictions,

THANK YOU FOR READING

BE SURE TO CHECK OUT ZACH MITCHELL'S OTHER PUBLISHED BOOKS ...

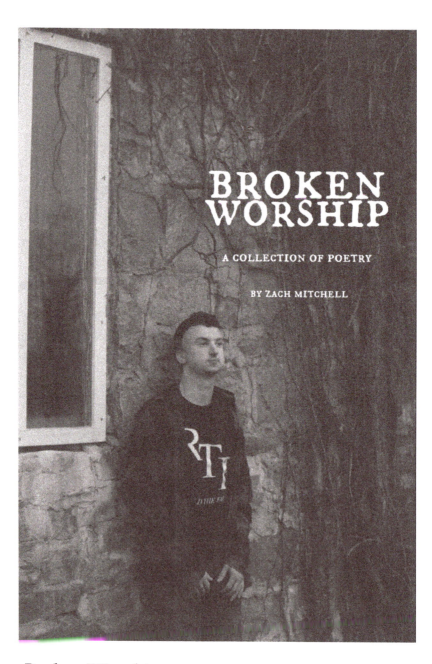

Broken Worship

Zach Mitchell's First Poetry Book

A COLLECTION OF POETRY
BY ZACH MITCHELL

No Darkness In Light

Zach Mitchell's Second Poetry Book

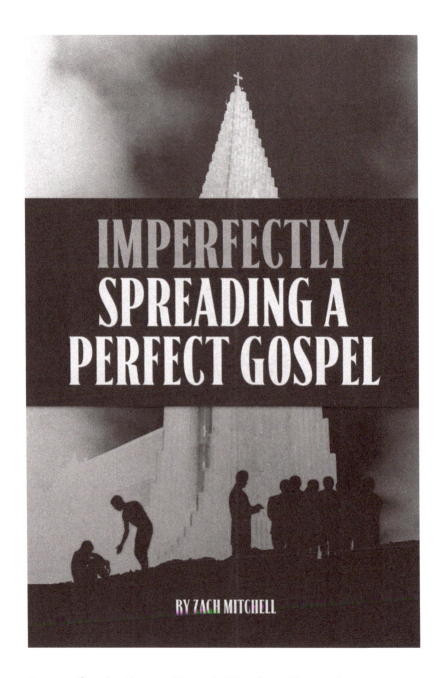

Imperfectly Spreading A Perfect Gospel

Zach Mitchell's First Chapter Book

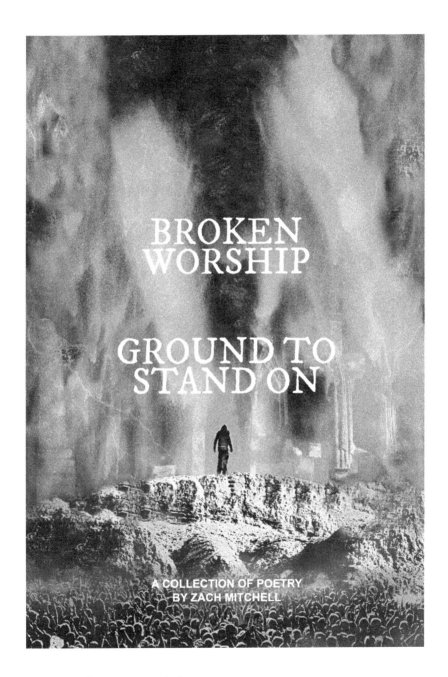

Ground To Stand On

Zach Mitchell's Third Poetry Book

Zach is also the founder and host of the Broken Worship Podcast. The Broken Worship Podcast is inspired by Zach's writing and faith. This podcast is based upon Zach's heart to reach broken and outcasted people to have faith. On his podcast, Zach discusses various topics relating to faith, music, and the Broken Worship Community. The heart of this podcast is in Zach's slogan, "Even in our brokenness, we have a reason to worship."

You can listen to the podcast via Spotify and YouTube!

You can learn more about Zach Mitchell and his Broken Worship Ministry at **www.broken-worship.com**

Thank you for reading and God bless!

CPSIA information can be obtained
at www.ICGtesting.com
Printed in the USA
BVHW050832110523
663998BV00003B/129